BLUE-COLLAR STRESS

ARTHUR B. SHOSTAK, PH.D.
Drexel University

BLUE-COLLAR STRESS

ADDISON-WESLEY PUBLISHING COMPANY

Reading, Massachusetts
Menlo Park, California • London
Amsterdam • Don Mills, Ontario • Sydney

This book is the third in the
Addison-Wesley Series on Occupational Stress

Library of Congress Cataloging in Publication Data

Shostak, Arthur B
   Blue-collar stress.

   (Occupational stress series ; 3)
   Includes bibliographical references and index.
   1. Job stress.   2. Labor and laboring classes.
I. Title.   II. Series.
HF5548.85.S48   301.44'42   79-16531
ISBN 0-201-07688-8

ISBN 0-201-07688-8
ABCDEFGHIJ-AL-79

This volume I dedicate with love and keen expectations to my young niece Sara and my three nephews, Daniel, Russell, and Eli, in the fond hope that no review of blue-collar workplace stress by a peer of theirs, years from now, will find so much in need of reform as does this slim volume of mine; between now and then I know they will do their part.

FOREWORD

The vast literature concerned with the individual coping with work stress stems from many and diverse disciplines, primarily psychiatry, clinical and social psychology, sociology, cultural anthropology, and occupational and internal medicine, with significant contributions from such widely different fields as behavioral toxicology and personnel and management. While each discipline is concerned with so-called "psychosocial stressors," communication between the several disciplines has generally been the exception rather than the rule. Lawyers, for example, tend to communicate mainly with other lawyers about the issues that concern them. Union leaders tend to communicate most often with other union leaders. Clinical psychologists direct their communications to their colleagues, but use a different language from that used by many of the psychiatrists who are equally concerned. Even social psychologists and industrial sociologists sometimes find it difficult to exchange data. The transfer of useful data from one discipline to another has proven to be very difficult. "Some researchers go about rediscovering the known, with little deference to an existing literature or to determinable frontiers for contemporary research; and what consensus may be possible is *not adequately disseminated for beneficial application beyond home base.*"*

* Robert Rose, editorial, *Journal of Human Stress*, Vol. 3 No. 1, March 1977.

Communication across disciplines is not the only difficulty that students of job-related stress encounter. Transcultural communication is a problem too. Western physiologists, for instance, who are concerned with hormones in the brain, have difficulty communicating with their eastern European colleagues who prefer to speak in terms of "higher nervous function."

There is growing common concern. Theories and practices in each discipline are beginning to cross-pollinate other disciplines and to exert a positive influence toward understanding the stresses of the workplace and workers' reactions.

The many denominators of concern for an employee population under stress form the unifying theme of these volumes. As a field of study, occupational stress is beginning to gel. It is a subject of increasing interest not only to members of unions and management, but also to the health professionals who serve as their consultants. Increasingly, awareness and expertise are being focused on both theoretical and practical problem solving. The findings of social scientists have led to the enactment of legislation in the Scandinavian countries, for instance, where employers are now required, under certain circumstances, to provide meaningful work and appropriate job satisfaction with a minimum of occupational stress.

The authors of these books represent many points of view and a variety of disciplines. Each, however, is interested in the same basic thing—greater job satisfaction and greater productivity for each employee. The books were written independently with only broad guidelines and coordination by the editor. Each is a unique, professional statement summarizing an area closely related to the main theme. Each extracts from that area applications which seem logically based on currently available knowledge.

All of the authors treat, from differing perspectives, three key concepts: stress, stressor, and stress reactions. *Stress* defines a process or a system which includes not only the stressful event and the reaction to it, but all the intervening steps between. The *stressor* is a stressful event or stressful condition that produces a psychological or physical reaction in the individual that is usually unpleasant and sometimes produces symptoms of emotional or physiological disability. The *stress reaction* concerns the consequences of the stimulus provided by a stressor. It is, in other words, the response to a stressor, and it is generally unhealthy. Most often, such reactions may be defined in rather traditional psychological terms, ranging from mild situational anxiety and depression to serious emotional disability.

Many frames of reference are represented in this series. A psychoanalyst describes the phenomenon of occupational stress in executives. A sociologist reflects the concern with blue-collar workers. Health-care-delivery systems and the prevention of occupational stress reactions are covered by occupational physicians. Other authors focus on social support systems and on physiological aspects of stress reactions. All the authors are equally concerned with the reduction of unhealthy environmental social stimuli both in the world of work and in the other aspects of life that the world of work affects. In each instance, the authors are concerned with defining issues and with drawing the kinds of conclusions that will suggest constructive solutions.

The legal system, beginning with worker's compensation statutes and more recently augmented by the Occupational Safety and Health Act, deals directly with occupational stress reactions and will be the subject of one of the books in the series. That statute, which created both the Occupational Safety and Health Administration and the National Institute for Occupational Safety and Health, contains a specific directive mandating study of psychologically stressful factors in the work environment. We have seen criteria documents and standards for physical factors in the work environment. We may soon see standards developed to govern acceptable levels of psychological stressors at work such as already exist in Sweden and Norway; another significant area of concern for this series.

At the beginning of this series it is difficult to foresee all the pivotal areas of interest which should be covered. It is even more difficult to predict the authors who will be able and willing to confront the issues as they emerge in the next few years. In a rapidly changing technological, scientific, and legislative world, the challenge will be to bring contemporary knowledge about occupational stress to an audience of intelligent managers who can translate thoughts into constructive action.

Alan A. McLean, M.D.
Editor

ACKNOWLEDGMENTS

New and old friends who have heard me out and traded ideas back and forth include Russ Allen of the AFL-CIO's George Meany Center for Labor Studies; Joe Barson, president of UAW Local 900, Flint, Michigan; William S. Hoffman of the Social Security Department of the UAW; Hy Kornblum of the University of Michigan; Ed Lawler III of the University of Michigan; Elliot Liebow of the Center for Metropolitan Studies, National Institute of Mental Health (NIMH); Oscar Paskel of UAW's Education Department; Lillian Rubin of the Institute for Scientific Analysis in San Francisco; and Donald Warren of Oakland University, Rochester, Michigan.

Christina Murianka, an old friend, was among the first to read early chapters and urge a pruning of verbiage, tables, and superfluities. Series editor Alan A. McLean read an early draft of oft-revised chapters and provided well-timed morale boosts when my confidence faltered. Michael Halperin, Head of the Reference Division of the Drexel University Library, gave invaluable backup support. A Drexel friend and colleague, Tom Childers, arranged for my authorized access to the project interview transcripts I had added to his 1976 research project on blue-collar information-seeking experiences.

Typing for the project was competently handled by Drexel secretary Eileen McLarnon, though the largest assignment went to an independent typist, Dorothy McGovern, who generously gave many valuable Christmas and spring days to help me meet deadline after deadline.

My parents, Milton and Betty Shostak, collected and stored hundreds of potential research aids (newspapers, magazines, and so on) over a period of several years, often at considerable personal inconvenience. Their anecdotes from their own worklives (my father, an independent neighborhood grocer for over thirty-three years; my mother, a nurse who has worked at a union health clinic), in combination with their analysis of nearly forty years of residence in the same Italian working-class community in Brooklyn (now a stress-marred "changing neighborhood"), lent much welcomed ballast to my own ideas about blue-collar realities and prospects.

Above all, however, this project's completion owes more than I can adequately and publicly express to my friend Lynn Seng, whose considerable editorial craft, *joie de vivre*, and thorough commitment to this endeavor has made all the difference . . . all the time.

Naturally, I alone am responsible for the volume's various short-comings, especially as I have made revisions without the benefit of consultation with my friends above, all of whom will understand, make notes, and hopefully join me in improving still-later revisions of this report years from now.

Philadelphia, Pennsylvania   A. B. S.
June 1979

If the employer or higher executive would spend a month every other year working as a humble worker in his own or some friend's plant, he would gain such insight into this problem of securing efficient administration of justice as to benefit greatly both himself and the workers, provided he left his preconceived ideas and prejudices behind.

REXFORD B. HERSEY

CONTENTS

INTRODUCTION

> *... the essential problems of men at work are the same whether they do their work in some famous laboratory or in the messiest vat room of a pickle factory.*
>
> EVERETT C. HUGHES*

Although written almost a half-century ago, Rex Hersey's 1932 volume, *Workers Emotions in Shop and Home*,[1] is an overlooked classic especially valuable in providing perspective on blue-collar workplace stress, its causes, and reactions. Drawing largely on his participant-observer research, Hersey emphasized the broad sweep of "sources of crises" then current in the lives of manual workers:

> *... the work itself, including the nature of the job, the amount accomplished, plant conditions, treatment by the foremen, relations with one's fellow workers, etc.; the physical condition of the worker, including a source which, for want of a better term, we may call "inside feeling"; outside causes, including relations with wife and children, influences of parents, success with girls, anticipation or memory of parties and other attempts at recreation, etc.; finances; and, finally, weather.*[2]

---

*"Work and Self," in E.C. Hughes, *The Sociological Eye: Selected Papers* (Chicago: Aldine-Atherton, 1971), p. 342.

Hersey's prognosis for planned efforts to reduce job-related stress was very encouraging:

> In any plant, at any time, some workers or executives or both are confronted with major crises which upset digestion, lower efficiency, and disturb emotional health. The cheering conclusion to be derived is that intelligent sympathy and understanding direction may prove of untold help.[3]

Revealingly enough, however, the successive deepening of the Depression of the 1930s put an end to Hersey's early innovations in antistress reforms. ("The world," Hersey warned, "is suffering [in 1932] from the efficiency complex and has forgotten that the purpose of production is the service of man.")[4]

Guided here forty-seven years later by the idea of stressors offered by the editor of this series, Alan A. McLean—those factors that produce fear, threaten one's self-esteem, and may stimulate feelings of losing control of one's self[5]—I explore my own 1979 version of Hersey's 1932 focus and ask, *What are the blue-collar "sources of crises" nowadays at work, and what might we do about them?* Like Hersey I also draw on my own participant-observer workplace research, beginning as a riveter in an airplane manufacturing plant in 1955 and extending through short stints as a union organizer, state wage-and-hour investigator, state mediation board intern, corporate consultant, and most often as a labor educator. Classes I have taught for the Rutgers University Labor Education Program; the Association of State, County, and Municipal Employees Union (New York City); and especially, the American Federation of Labor and Congress of Industrial Organizations' (AFL-CIO) George Meany Center for Labor Studies (Silver Spring, Maryland) have taught me much that I try to incorporate into this volume, as has also twenty-five years of formal study and college teaching of industrial and labor relations subjects.

If I were pressed to single out one resource as more significant than all others, however, it would be the informal, off-the-record conversations I have enjoyed with blue-collar friends over the course of my lifetime, going back to my early years in a Brooklyn blue-collar neighborhood and coming up-to-date through my twelve years of ongoing teaching at Drexel University, a "red brick" blue-collar (and lower-middle-class) institution.

FOCUS AND COVERAGE

In 1961 I wrote my first blue-collar study, *America's Forgotten Labor Organization*, in which I argued that at least one-third of the forty-five single-firm independent unions I studied did not deserve the disdain of those who blithely assumed all such unions were company dominated. In 1964 I coedited a volume entitled *New Perspectives on Poverty*, in which my essays argued that many in the working class lived lives of more stress and grimmer prospects than outsiders seemed to realize or give a damn about. In 1965 I coedited a collection of sixty-four essays entitled *Blue-Collar World*, and most recently, in 1968, I wrote a monograph, *Blue-Collar Life*, in which I concluded that "America's working class is one that fears to dare, figures small angles incompetently, and makes the least-best of its life-enhancing possibilities." Blue-collarites, I added, are very much in trouble, as "too much at present has too many members of the working class making too little of their lives."[6]

I mention these earlier books to make the point that far too little is known about the American working class, and dialogue here *must* be strengthened if we are to improve the stress record in this matter soon. Levinson is correct, in my opinion, when he spotlights a remarkable blind spot in our national consciousness:

> The truth is that working-class people are shadowy figures to most middle-class people. Contact is limited to a quick glance at a knot of construction workers sitting on the sidewalk eating lunch. Or else it is a few words exchanged with a postman, doorman, or telephone installer. Beyond this, few have gone.[7]

Accordingly, I move cautiously, taking little for granted about a reader's familiarity with deceptive, veiled, and changing aspects of the private workplace world of manual workers.

In the spring of 1976, for example, I participated in a small-scale study sponsored by the Department of Health, Education, and Welfare (HEW) that helped to shed valuable new light for me on this subject. Interviews were conducted with fifty Caucasian blue-collar families in two ethnic enclaves (Irish and Italian) in Philadelphia working-class neighborhoods; this material was buttressed by a thorough study of the research literature available on America's 40 million manual workers.[8] Our study documented a remarkable amount of benefit inadequacies, health maladies and bills, home and family strains, and financial obligations and risks. Typical are these (reconstructed) excerpts from interviews I conducted:

Fred Armond, 11th grade education, married, 2 children, 28-year-old laborer: *The prices ... the prices for houses kill me. ... Naturally, the goddamn car is also falling apart at the same time. I lost a day's pay last week when I had to stay home all day and work on it. ... I don't make more than $13,000 in a good year, and I just can't keep up with it! The prices of everything are too high; my wife won't let me come along anymore when she shops for the week because I bitch so much; I can't say as I blame her. ... Hell, she tells everybody I'm a real "Archie Bunker," and where the dumb colored and the goddamn inflation are concerned, she is goddamn right!!*

Paul Kingman, 11th grade education, single, 21-year-old produce handler: *My biggest worry recently probably has been my mother's operations and whether or not my old man's union medical benefits would cover the costs. She was actually refused by a nonmember hospital, and we had to shop around to get her into a place that accepts the union plan ... everything depends on your coverage, so poor people get shafted! We've got three incomes in this house, and about $23,000 coming in, so we can swing it, but the others, they get shafted! ... My job is also a pain in the ass. They've made me a foreman, almost, and there is just too much aggravation and nervous tension in my life. I am too young to be telling people as old as my father what to do!*

Louis Aaron, 7th grade education, married, 3 children, 64-year-old pressman: *What sorts of things are bothering me? We have no more overtime, for one thing, so I can't pull in my $12,000 anymore; I'm earning under $10,000 now, after 35 years as a pressman, and while I'm living good, when I go on retirement I won't be able to do the things I want to — like go fishing and crabbing. ... I paid a guy $250 to have my roof fixed, and he robbed me! He said he made a mistake, but he never came back to fix it! I borrowed the money from my daughter-in-law and do not want to tell my sons I was gypped. They'll make a big commotion, and maybe break the guy's arms and legs. I don't know what to do about this anymore. ...*

Hal Highman, high school graduate, married, childless, 26-year-old electrician: *I need better information about unemployment benefits. I think the contractor has broken his word to me, and I wonder if there is any union or legal remedy so this won't happen again . . . you see, I stay on unemployment a half year every year and work on improving myself. I take psych courses, audio courses, work on my stock investments, take care of my organic garden, practice my pilot skills, and do a lot with the boy scouts. Meanwhile, my wife teaches school, and we both practice avoiding housework. . . .*

Overall, then, my (renamed) interviewees—Fred, Paul, Louis, and Hal—appear to share stressors well-known throughout American society, but which seem to be more sharply felt and less adequately met here than in more affluent social classes. These major sources of stress, often hidden from scrutiny by outsiders, will receive frank and searching attention throughout.

Now, as for the volume's exclusions, two in particular must be understood before we can get on with the matter: First, it is neither feasible nor advisable to attempt to discuss *all* the nation's 40 million manual workers, and a critical differentiation I make narrows the focus of my book profoundly (more on this below). Second, it is neither feasible nor advisable to attempt to draw work stress comparisons among the nation's various social classes. That task plainly demands many more pages than this volume permits, and considerably more knowledge than I command of the various classes; for example, old money rich and nouveau riche; upper middle, middle middle, lower middle; and welfare poor, working poor, and chronic poor are some of the divisions, to say nothing of those inside the working class itself.

As for the differentiation that I make among three types of blue-collarites—that is, white males, nonwhite males, and all females—I have chosen to focus only on the largest single group of manual workers, approximately 25 million *white males*. The literature on stress and blue-collarites offers very little at present on over 3 million nonwhite manual workers or on some 12 million female manual workers of any race. Additions are steadily being made to help close the manifold research gaps here, but the material now on hand encourages separate discussion of the races and the sexes:

Julius Shiskin, Commissioner of Labor Statistics: ... *the two [racial] groups are on two different tracks, with the whites enjoying the benefits of this economic expansion and the blacks not doing so ... we have a two-track economy, very different problems for whites and blacks. ... They have been drifting farther apart.*[9]

Nancy Seiffer, Director of the Center on Women and American Diversity: ... [*in 1975*] *the major research done on a group that represented over half the women in America was over a decade old, which meant that it predated the new Women's Movement. It portrayed working class women as passive, dependent, and uninvolved in the outside world. I had first hand evidence to the contrary ... there was a great void. In the rush of new literature inspired by the feminist movement, there was hardly a mention of working class women.*[10]

The situation of nonwhite males then, set off as it is by historic occupational racism and contemporary turmoil (via affirmative action programs), along with the comparable condition of female blue-collarites, plainly requires separate, detailed, and lengthy exploration ... in a book other than this.

Even while narrowing my volume's focus to the occupational stressors of white male blue-collarites, I have expanded its coverage to include a large bloc of "service workers" that are sometimes mistakenly identified as "white-collarites." The workers at issue here include porters, janitors, waiters, elevator operators, cooks, watchmen, barbers, and numerous others whose occupations, while not stereotypical factory or warehouse production and distribution jobs, essentially involve rote manual labor. Hereafter, the term "blue-collar" will refer to *white males* employed as *craftsmen* (carpenters, machinists, repairmen, painters, etc.); *operatives* (assemblers, welders, deliverymen, truck drivers, etc.); *service workers* (except sales personnel); and *laborers* (lumbermen, longshoremen, fishermen, etc., but not including farm workers).

LAYOUT AND EMPHASIS

To better discipline what otherwise could prove overwhelming in scope and detail, I have arranged a seven-part layout for this volume. Chapter 1 explores four objective stressors (compensation, health and safety hazards, conditions in the workplace, and the fact or threat of unemployment), while Chapter 2 focuses on four subjective stressors (status, supervision, sociability, and job satisfaction). Chapters 3 and 4 deal with selected aspects of the local union and international union scene, respectively, and explore how manual workers "experience" labor as an aid, though sometimes also as a bane, where workplace stressors are concerned.

Guided in part by the contention of series editor Alan A. McLean that "there is far more psychopathology coming from outside events than from those related to the work itself,"[11] I have prepared two additional chapters on selected aspects of the after-work life of blue-collarites: Chapter 5 studies workplace links to the workers' physical and mental health, and Chapter 6 explores blue-collar fears that job losses may follow from environmental protection measures. Blue-collar ambiguity about the stress-reducing ways to go in the years ahead is especially clear and pointed in this headline matter.

Finally, I use the volume's epilogue to explore selected aspects of the near future in this matter. A small number of uncertain possibilities are discussed, all of them guided by Wolf's law: "It isn't that things will necessarily go wrong (Murphy's law), but rather they will take so much more time and effort than you think, if they are not to."[12]

At three points in the volume I offer material prepared by trade unionists who stood out as students of mine in college-level sociology courses I have been teaching recently at the AFL-CIO's George Meany Center for Labor Studies. These men, Andrew A. Cuvo, Kenneth W. Yunger, and Gary Spencer, are especially insightful and straightforward in their brief essays that I reprint; rich hours of uninhibited and often heated classroom dialogue with talented unionists like Gary, Ken, and Andrew have influenced this entire volume.

Another all-chapter influence of note concerns the origin of a distinctive feature with which nearly every chapter closes: Twenty-five years of involvement with executives, managers, foremen, and almost every level of the labor hierarchy has left me deeply impressed with the keen interest *all* show in workplace reform possibilities. To be sure, this line of inquiry is tempered by the sort of experience-grounded insights evident in the sage advice of management consultant Dr. Ralph Siu:

> There is no such thing as an occupational stress problem which can be solved for all time and forgotten about, like a mathematical

.

problem of two plus two equals four. There are only occupational stress issues — never fully delineated, never completely resolved, always changing, always in need of alert accommodation.[13]

Guided then by the conviction that there are no ultimate answers or final truths, only the situationally appropriate amelioration of selected stressors, I have made a special effort to explore a fairly large and diverse selection of antistress reform possibilities.

The criteria by which I chose some reforms for inclusion and excluded others involved their seeming promise, their apparent freshness, and wherever possible, their evidence of successful operation, even if only in a small-scale case-study fashion. Above all, I paid attention to a point made earlier by Robert Caplan and associates: "In the long run our aim is to find ways of preventing job stresses from impacting upon the worker — rather than ways of developing a better tranquilizer for the resulting strains."[14] In a strategic and constructive fashion this characterizes *the* major goal of this entire volume, namely, to get out ahead of blue-collar workplace stressors in a practical and profitable way to better help reduce our need for tranquilizers — for all of us, blue-collarites and others.

NOTES

1. Rexford B. Hersey, *Workers' Emotions in Shop and Home: A Study of Individual Workers from the Psychological and Physiological Standpoint* (Philadelphia: University of Pennsylvania Press, 1932).

2. *Ibid.*, p. 32-33. See also E. Wright Bakke, *Management in the Course of Industrialization* (New York: Harper Torchbooks, 1963); Carroll M. Brodsky, *The Harassed Worker* (Lexington, MA: Lexington Books, 1976); Iradj Saissi, *et al.*, "Loneliness and Dissatisfaction in a Blue Collar Population," *Archives of General Psychiatry* 30 (February 1974): 261-265; Teresa A. Sullivan, *Marginal Workers, Marginal Jobs: The Underutilization of American Workers* (Austin: University of Texas Press, 1978); Cary L. Cooper and Roy Payne, *Stress at Work* (New York: Wiley, 1978).

3. Hersey, *op cit.*, p. 301. Hersey advised that if economists and businessmen could produce the necessary machinery to "make our consumption needs effective," then "the industrial psychologist can work out the organization and technique for calling forth the necessary efficiency without *always* holding a whip over the workers' or executives' heads" (p. 304). To the psychologist, Hersey added, increased production, like happiness, must be a by-product of an improved adjustment of the worker — at work, home, and play. See also John Koten, "Career Guidance: Psychologists Play Bigger Corporate Role in Placing of Personnel," *Wall Street Journal*, July 11, 1978, pp. 1, 29.

4. Hersey, *op cit.*, p. 304. See also Roy P. Fairfield, ed., *Humanizing the Workplace* (New York: Prometheus Books, 1974); John Julian Ryan,

"Humanistic Work: Its Philosophical and Cultural Implications," in W. J. Heisler and John W. Houck, eds., *A Matter of Dignity: Inquiries into the Humanization of Work* (Notre Dame, IN: University of Notre Dame Press, 1977).

5. Alan A. McLean, *Work Stress* (Reading, MA: Addison-Wesley, 1979). See especially Chapter 1, "The Stress of Work," p. 1-16.

6. Arthur Shostak, *Blue Collar Life* (New York: Random House, 1969), pp. 290-291. See also Arthur Shostak and W. Gomberg, eds., *Blue-Collar World* (Englewood Cliffs, NJ: Prentice-Hall, 1965); Arthur Shostak and W. Gomberg, eds., *New Perspectives on Poverty* (Englewood Cliffs, NJ: Prentice-Hall, 1964); Arthur Shostak, *America's Forgotten Labor Organization* (Princeton, NJ: Industrial Relations Section, Princeton University, 1962).

7. Andrew Levinson, *The Working-Class Majority* (New York: Penguin, 1975), p. 43.

8. See in this connection Thomas Childers and Joyce Post, *The Blue Collar Adult's Information Needs, Seeking Behavior and Use* (Washington, DC: HEW, Office of Education, March 1976). I and my colleagues interviewed fifty workers in their Philadelphia homes during the spring of 1976. With a small grant of $37,000 from the Office of Education, the Office of Libraries and Learning Resources, and HEW, as secured by a friend, Dr. Thomas Childers of the Library School faculty at Drexel University, we sought to study the information needs, information-seeking behavior, and information use of the blue-collar adult—in order to help HEW formulate library policy in connection with this particular type of citizen.

9. Julius Shiskin, "The Labor Market: Matching Up the Statistics and the Realities," *Challenge*, January-February 1978, pp. 31-32. See also Duane E. Leigh, *An Analysis of Determinants of Occupational Upgrading* (New York: Academic Press, 1978).

10. Nancy Seifer, *Nobody Speaks for Me! Self-Portraits of American Working Class Women* (New York: Simon and Schuster, 1976), p. 25. See also Barbara M. Wertheimer and Anne H. Nelson, *Trade Union Women: A Study of Their Participation in New York City Locals* (New York: Praeger 1975); Louise Kapp Howe, *Pink Collar Workers: Inside the World of Women's Work* (New York: Avon, 1977); "The Hardships that Blue Collar Women Face," *Business Week*, August 14, 1978, p. 90; "The Deep Discontent of the Working Woman," *Business Week*, February 5, 1979, pp. 28-29.

11. As quoted in Pasquale A. Carone, *et al.*, eds., *The Emotionally Troubled Employee: A Challenge to Industry* (Albany: State University of New York Press, 1976), p. 28.

12. As quoted in Paul Dickson, *The Official Rules* (New York: Delacorte Press, 1978), p. 188.

13. R.G.H. Siu, "The Tao of Organization Management," Chapter 14 in Alan A. McLean, ed., *Reducing Occupational Stress*, National Institute for Occupational Safety and Health, DHEW-NIOSH pub. no. 78-140 (April 1978), p. 136.

14. Robert D. Caplan, *et al.*, *Job Demands and Worker Health: Main Effects and Occupational Differences* (Washington, DC: HIOSH Research Report, Government Printing Office, 1975), p. 1. For criticism of reforms that would have social science play a controlling role in the future of work see Joseph C. Mouledoux and Elizabeth C. Mouledoux, *Alienation: A Critical Evaluation of Selected Empirical Studies* (Montreal: Societe Canadienne de Sociologie et d'Anthropologie [Canadian Sociology and Anthropology Association], 1974).

1

BLUE-COLLAR WORK: OBJECTIVE FACTORS

I wondered why people made such a mad dash to get out of the plant when they knew they were destined to be stuck in long, unpleasant lines of cars. People offered a number of explanations, reflecting a deep feeling of relief when a day of work is finished, and an anxiousness to leave the plant. Whatever the reason, once that bell rang, people wanted to get out of the plant no matter what.

RICHARD BALZER*

Potential workplace stressors of a hard-nosed variety, the kind you can almost touch, see, feel, or hear (in contrast to the softer, really more subjective matters I discuss in the next chapter) are essentially four—a man's pay, a man's safety at work, the quality of his work setting, and the stability of his job. White male blue-collarites I interviewed for this volume, along with many others reported on in the literature, regularly raised questions about their income, the risks they ran at work, the nature of the workplace, and the likelihood of having any work at all in the foreseeable future, or possibly even tomorrow. These four stressors, or the complex issues entailed in *compensation*, *health* and *safety hazards*, *work setting*, and *work loss*, are discussed

---

*Richard Balzer, *Clockwork: Life in and Outside an American Factory* (Garden City, NY: Doubleday, 1976). p. 18.

in some detail below to better provide a meaningful background later for the chapter's reform possibilities.

COMPENSATION

Whether interviewing in blue-collar households, informally talking with union officers or "reps" at the AFL-CIO's George Meany Labor Center, or chatting with workers in factories or roadside truckstops, I have been struck by the special character of their compensation criticisms. While few rail about dollar levels per se, many rely instead on a much more complicated critique of their own earnings situation.

There is nothing very mysterious about this, once its defensive nature is better understood:

- Self-esteem protection recommends that each of us maintain a positive notion of ourself as an "adequate" provider.

- Inflationary dollars result in gross wage levels nowadays in very large numbers, over $1,000 a month for many, a sum certainly larger than any ever earned years ago (or ever earned by one's blue-collar father); and this props up the illusion of economic well-being.

- Male blue-collarites are frequently shielded from the full story of their own family's economic stringency by wives who want to spare them "additional worries."

- Male blue-collarites learn from decades of experience to mute and even deny dissatisfaction with stressors that seem out of their hands, that they have little clear hope of reforming.

In short, as many of the men explained to me over and again, "It's more than I ever expected to be earning . . . and so, it's just *got* to do."

At the same time, of course, compensation actually connects to stressors that are fully as vexing and complex as any known in blue-collar lives. Six major stress reactions here include:

- The struggle not to lose ground to inflation's erosion of purchasing power

- The fear that "cures" for inflation may prove more costly for blue-collarites than the ill itself

- The discomfort over being blamed for the wage-price spiral

- The irregular character of nonsalaried compensation

- The anxieties that accompany the jockeying for position among jealous blue-collar occupations

- The ambivalence that accompanies reliance on compensation gains through "category" bargaining wins rather than through individual effort

These six stressors, especially when they operate in tandem, profoundly undercut the otherwise superficial aura of economic well-being suggested by absolute high levels of pay (*before* taxes), the growth of fringes (*before* qualifications), and the glut of consumer goods ownership (*before* the bills come in).

More revealing yet, the unholy six provoke an unsuccessful attempt at a stress reducing mechanism which will repeat again and again throughout this book: Large numbers of blue-collarites struggle—unsuccessfully—to locate blame for their plight somewhere other than in themselves. Unconvinced by their own efforts, however, many wind up pointing the finger at themselves and retreat into lives marred by considerable self-blame and malaise.

Keeping up with . . . everybody

Blue-collarites, as relatively newly-arrived, bottom-rung claimants to lower-middle-class status, are sorely strained to maintain their very precarious perch. Accordingly, working-class wives are disproportionately represented among the ranks of married women at work. Older children still living in blue-collar homes as young adults are expected to contribute liberally to pooled family income. Overtime is welcomed by most, and moonlighting is commonplace (though many resent its tax on their stamina and on their family time together).

Despite these sorts of vigorous income-boosting efforts, the economic unease of the blue-collarite grows greater all the (inflation-fed) time: From 1946-56, for example, the average real take-home pay of manufacturing workers with three dependents rose about 2 percent per year. From 1956-66, gains slowed slightly to 1.4 percent, but from 1966 to 1976, gains plummeted to 0.3 percent. Even this calculation, however, may *overstate* blue-collar purchasing power, for when translated into 1976 price levels, the annual gain in the 1966-76 decade worked out to about $5.66 a week, of which nearly $4.00 went into higher state and local taxes: "For workers in many areas, the rise in local taxation may very well have meant no rise at all in disposable income over the past ten years."[1]

Not surprisingly, then, a union staffer, when recently asked to defend labor's bargaining demands, explained that "the only thing that affects demands is when you look at what it costs to live. You're not doing your job unless you at least try to get in there and keep up."[2]

Cures can kill!

Workers know much about inflation as a stressor, especially as the nation's price level has been virtually an exponential curve since 1965, and has increased at an average of more than 9 percent per year since 1972—faster than for any comparable time span since the First World War.[3] Workers have lost purchasing power and discretionary income, as well as having fallen behind median income levels. The dollar's lack of reliable value has led to the suspicion that someone or something is fooling, manipulating, and cheating them. Many whom I've talked with about this are increasingly persuaded that no reformer can make any desirable reform impact here, at least in the near future.

Over and above the present-day toll exacted by persistent inflation, blue-collarites also worry about likely remedies now favored by various politicians. The director of the government's Council on Wage and Price Stability concurs:

> The most realistic threat the country faces is not controls, but another recession. We can see the signs already. . . . A recession is likely because that has always been the government's anti-inflation policy.[4]

Again, while few workers will know the details, many can intuit the considerable hazard to their well-being represented in this erstwhile reform equation: Achieving a drop of 1 percent point in the inflation rate through macroeconomic policy may entail a 2-point, *2-million person increase in the unemployment rate* (and a loss of $100 billion worth of output).[5]

Resenting a "bum rap"

Blue-collarites are especially bitter about the blame directed their way by nonunionists looking to scapegoat the *cause* of the inflationary spiral. Machinist Union President William W. Winpisinger explains:

> There is a very definite rightward tilt to the thinking of the country today, and the twenty-, thirty-year campaign of our enemies to discredit us [in labor] has paid handsome dividends in recent years. They've more and more made union members the villains

*of the number one problem afflicting the American people—and
that's the inflationary spiral eroding the ability to live decently.
Union members get a lion's share of the blame for this. Even some
of them become convinced that they might be culprits.*[6]

In defense, spokesmen like the AFL-CIO head George Meany never
tire of pointing out that "every study that has been made ... has
indicated that the inflation that we're going through is not due to
wages. . . . wage settlements are a reflection of a condition that already
exists."[7] *Business Week* concurs, and advises its audience that "union
leaders are largely correct in claiming that wage increases have not
caused inflation in a cost-push sense."[8] Nevertheless, hostility toward
labor, and thereby toward the workingman (and woman), remains
constant and high.

Blue-collar "income averaging"

Hired by the hour, the day, or possibly by the job, many blue-collarites become intimately familiar with the ups and downs of irregular
earning and employment, though few ever find much to appreciate
about this sort of unpredictability.

In a frank moment of troubled self-review, a veteran ironworker
explains his "roller coaster" income history in this way:

> *"I made sixteen t'ousand dollars last year," he said, "and eleven
> and a half t'e year before last. But, t'e year before I made less t'an
> six, and I bet if you averaged out my whole ironworkin' life, it
> wouldn't come to eight. I pay t'ree times what a regular person
> does for a little bit of life insurance, and I get no pension, and
> when my beat-up body starts to slow down it'll be harder to get
> work, and if I lose even just a hand, I'm t'rough on t'e spot.
> Sometimes I t'ink if t'e niggers and P.R.'s want t'e stinkin' trade,
> t'ey can have it."* [9]

Similarly, a crane operator conveys his impatience with the public's
misimpression:

> *In the winter time, sometimes you're off several months. People
> will say, look at the money this man's making. But when other
> people are working, he's getting nothing. In the steel mill, when
> they get laid off, they get so much money per week for so many
> weeks. When I get laid off, there's nothing more than to get
> another job. We have no paid holidays, no paid vacations.*[10]

White-collarites I've talked with, especially those on annual salaries and uninterrupted fringe benefit plans, often find these sorts of compensation conditions hard to comprehend . . . or accept. (College president John R. Coleman, assessing his $2.40 an hour weekly take in 1973 while working temporarily as a kitchen helper, concluded he could probably scrape by on it as a single man if he had to, but "it would just be to keep alive and not really live."[11])

Who's on first?

Workers look down resentfully on a welfare class that seems to steadily and unfairly gain on them ("unfairly" translates as "through no real effort of their own"). They also look enviously above at the compensation extras of top company executives (see Table 1).

TABLE 1   *Executive compensation "perks."*

Perquisites	Percentage of 468 major corporations granting benefit
Executive physicals	83
Spouse traveling on company business	79
Company cars	62
Luncheon-club memberships	55
Country-club memberships	53
Extended vacations	38
Company airplanes	37
Company apartments, suites	22

Source: Survey conducted by Hay-Huggins, a division of Hay Associates; as reported in *Business Week*, March 27, 1978, p. 34.

Similarly, the feature story in a representative union newspaper, *Allied Industrial Worker*, for January 1979, relates this news to rank-and-filers:

> *A survey of nearly 1,500 companies has found that the pay of top executives rose sharply over the last two years, with base salaries increasing between 16 and 20%. Median compensation (salary plus bonus) was $241,000 for chief executives in manufacturing in 1978, the Conference Board, a business-oriented research group, reported (p. 1).*

Closer to home, blue-collarites remain jealous of better-educated middle-class families that seem to pull steadily ahead—whether in fact or fiction not really making much of a difference.

Provoked by these stressors, blue-collar males never stop measuring their income situation against significant others in their own ranks, each cluster of workers (electricians versus butchers versus cabbies versus carpenters, etc.) anxious to preserve its hard-earned and precious status in the working-class pecking order (see Table 2).

TABLE 2 *Blue-collar earnings: comparative picture*

Occupational type	After-tax income†		Change in income after taxes and effects of inflation
	1967	1978	
Plumber	$9,515	$18,045*	+ 4.5%
Petrochemical worker	$7,163	$17,027	+22%
Steelworker	$6,580	$16,932	+32%
Auto worker	$6,670	$16,114	+24%

† Assuming three dependents.

*1977

Source: The Tax Foundation, Inc., as reported in *Time*, January 15, 1979, p. 59.

As is true of *all* of America's social classes, various components of the class jealously measure income and prestige differences among themselves with exacting calibration: Typical is the rivalry of the skilled craftsmen versus all others in the Auto Workers Union (UAW). A classic illustration of keenly valued differentials *within* the working class, this feud pivots on pay differentials of craft workers that gall the hell out of the union's semiskilled and unskilled plurality. Negotiations are regularly marred by low-level rumbling that occasionally erupts into major internecine battles.

This jockeying for position occurs throughout the entire blue-collar category, as illustrated by these comments:

Heavy equipment operator: *You take the other crafts, like an ironworker, he needs a belt, two spud wrenches, a knife which costs him fifteen dollars, and he makes more than a crane operator. The crane operator, he's responsible for a machine that cost over a quarter of a million dollars. Regardless of what kind of machine it is, they all cost anywhere from thirty-five, forty thousand dollars and up. So why isn't he worth as much money?*[12]

> Labor relations director at an electrical manufacturing plant: *At some of our plants we have highly trained, skilled guys who live in the same neighborhood as auto workers and steelworkers, but make no more than a broom pusher in an auto or steel plant. That gives us all kinds of trouble.*[13]

Competition of this sort, which keeps men divided from one another all of their work lives (and even into pension-comparing retirement), taxes the working class in a remarkable, albeit covert, fashion that cannot be overestimated in impact . . . or so my blue-collar friends persuade me.

Winning on my own!

As if the foregoing were not enough, additional distress can be traced to a little-recognized source, the *group* nature of blue-collar income gains. Socialist economist Joan Robinson explains that society pays a special price when earnings are predicated on group membership:

> *When it becomes clear that the relative incomes of individuals are mainly determined by the bargaining position of the group to which they belong, the ethics of the system—a fair day's work for a fair day's wage—disintegrates, industrial discipline is undermined, and the tradition of public services gives way to a general scramble for advantage.*[14]

With regard to blue-collar stress, what vexes many, then, is the fact that income gains are *collective* ones, that what is won by a worker is generally won through union negotiations on behalf of *all* workers, or by employer grants to *all*, and has no particular tie to an individual's merit or need.

Why should this be a source of stress? And a veiled one, at that? Because "the code of respect running through all these people's lives demands that a man 'make something of himself,' that he justify his material gains by a *personal* effort" (italics added).[15] Workers are nevertheless obliged to bargain *en masse*. Many are left terribly ambivalent, therefore, about their individual merits as compared to how they feel about their collective prowess: Gains are discounted to the extent that they derive from merely belonging to a category (such as "unionist" or "welfare recipient"). Only as one exerts some personal control, only as one occasionally singles oneself out for significant reward, can one escape the feeling of powerlessness and personal insignificance otherwise embedded in contemporary blue-collar lives.

This particularly debilitating stressor is left in the
agreement of all.

HEALTH AND SAFETY HAZARDS

On a scale of nineteen possible workplace sources of job discontent,
the second highest choice, topped only by compensation, was health
and safety hazards—or so thought a nationwide sample of workers
polled in 1971 by the Labor Department.[16] The same results were
secured by the Institute for Social Research (ISR) in a 1972-73 study,
and my discussions with workers have persuaded me that they are
likely to turn up again if the question was put today to the nation's
blue-collarites.

Over 14,000 workers die annually in industrial accidents (nearly
55 a day, or 7 people every working hour), over 100,000 workers are
permanently disabled every year, and employers report more than 5
million occupational injuries annually. Stress here is due even more to
new anxieties stirred by almost weekly revelations of the "silent violence of occupational diseases." Television news programs and hour-
long television specials advise millions of viewers nationwide that—

- as many as 14 million workers are exposed daily to dangerous
  toxic materials that occupational health specialists remain uncertain about; and—

- perhaps 600,000 workers are already into a danger phase from past
  exposure to cancer-causing workplace materials.

Little wonder that a concerned U.S. Senator, Jacob Javits (R-NY),
asked by television reporters to capsulize the situation, sighed and
warned, "We are in deep trouble in this nation."[17]

New research-based estimates of the toll of workplace chemicals,
radiation, heat stress, pesticides, fumes, and other toxic matters leads
the National Institute of Occupational Safety and Health (NIOSH) to
estimate that about 100,000 workers may die annually (and often
horribly) from industrial diseases that *could* have been prevented. As
well, an additional 300,000 may contract disabling occupation-based
diseases, also preventable, over the same twelve months.[18] When
NIOSH in 1975 studied the medical illnesses of a sample of workers in
unprecedented depth, it concluded that 81 percent "probably were
caused by their jobs, and another 10 percent might have been." [19]

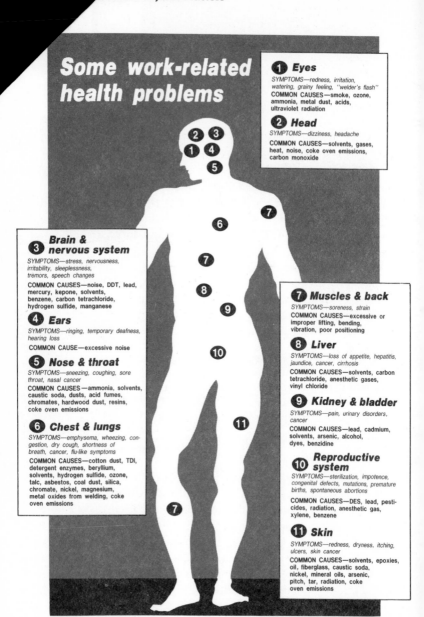

Some work-related health problems

1 Eyes

SYMPTOMS—redness, irritation, watering, grainy feeling, "welder's flash"

COMMON CAUSES—smoke, ozone, ammonia, metal dust, acids, ultraviolet radiation

2 Head

SYMPTOMS—dizziness, headache

COMMON CAUSES—solvents, gases, heat, noise, coke oven emissions, carbon monoxide

3 Brain & nervous system

SYMPTOMS—stress, nervousness, irritability, sleeplessness, tremors, speech changes

COMMON CAUSES—noise, DDT, lead, mercury, kepone, solvents, benzene, carbon tetrachloride, hydrogen sulfide, manganese

4 Ears

SYMPTOMS—ringing, temporary deafness, hearing loss

COMMON CAUSE—excessive noise

5 Nose & throat

SYMPTOMS—sneezing, coughing, sore throat, nasal cancer

COMMON CAUSES—ammonia, solvents, caustic soda, dusts, acid fumes, chromates, hardwood dust, resins, coke oven emissions

6 Chest & lungs

SYMPTOMS—emphysema, wheezing, congestion, dry cough, shortness of breath, cancer, flu-like symptoms

COMMON CAUSES—cotton dust, TDI, detergent enzymes, beryllium, solvents, hydrogen sulfide, ozone, talc, asbestos, coal dust, silica, chromate, nickel, magnesium, metal oxides from welding, coke oven emissions

7 Muscles & back

SYMPTOMS—soreness, strain

COMMON CAUSES—excessive or improper lifting, bending, vibration, poor positioning

8 Liver

SYMPTOMS—loss of appetite, hepatitis, jaundice, cancer, cirrhosis

COMMON CAUSES—solvents, carbon tetrachloride, anesthetic gases, vinyl chloride

9 Kidney & bladder

SYMPTOMS—pain, urinary disorders, cancer

COMMON CAUSES—lead, cadmium, solvents, arsenic, alcohol, dyes, benzidine

10 Reproductive system

SYMPTOMS—sterilization, impotence, congenital defects, mutations, premature births, spontaneous abortions

COMMON CAUSES—DES, lead, pesticides, radiation, anesthetic gas, xylene, benzene

11 Skin

SYMPTOMS—redness, dryness, itching, ulcers, skin cancer

COMMON CAUSES—solvents, epoxies, oil, fiberglass, caustic soda, nickel, mineral oils, arsenic, pitch, tar, radiation, coke oven emissions

Chicago Sun-Times Graphic by Jack Jordon

Not surprisingly, many blue-collar workplaces seethe with nerve-wracking rumors of alleged ill health consequences from this or that daily work process or exposure. Workers suspect a gamut of possible disabilities ranging from premature baldness and sexual impotence to lung disease and cancer deaths; whether imaginary or real, the stress toll here is enormous. (Workers I have known talk like walking medical dictionaries, somewhat in the fashion of jailhouse lawyers; while aware of unevenness in their medical insight, they nevertheless serve as "lay medics" of considerable impact on their shop's stress quotient.)

Fatalism, of course, has always helped temper the worker's response to a workplace hazard, as in this revealing account of a kitchen crew's reaction to a coworker's debilitating accident:

> *Everyone is agreed tonight that he is lucky to have a foot at all. Everyone is also agreed that the [kitchen] elevator is a menace and that something should be done about it. Everyone is agreed finally that nothing will be done; they should act, but "they" won't. Someday there will be a serious accident and a state investigation. Things will change at last. Meanwhile, we'll all cluck our tongues, be a bit more careful for a few days, and then go on as usual.*[20]

Similarly, a baker who wears a hearing aid to help relieve his deafness calmly recalls its occupational origins:

> *I lost my hearing while working at [an airplane manufacturing company], around the jet engines. There were about forty of them testing all over the place. You don't feel a thing. All you hear is the deafening noise. It gets so that you don't even hear that—you don't think about it. There's no pain involved in loss of hearing, it's just something that catches up to you. It caught up to me a couple of years after I was out there. I'd keep asking my family, "What'd you say? What'd you say? Turn the TV up a little louder," and it's knocking everybody's ears out.*[21]

A bricklayer, in turn, chooses to accent the positive:

> *We aren't far enough ahead financially to be able to cope with anything really big. Like last spring, a pair of bricks fell off a platform and broke my left wrist. I couldn't lay bricks for four months. Fortunately, I was able to do laboring work, and being in a family business, my father and brother helped carry me through. But if I had broken a leg, where I couldn't have even labored, we would have been very bad off.*[22]

Workman's compensation benefits, unemployment insurance . . . all
are relatively well-known to blue-collarites, and their red tape and
inadequate financial benefits come in for strong denunciation whenever the subject earns workplace discussion.

Many workers learn to combine a hard-boiled veneer about job
hazards with abiding private anxieties, as in this vignette of public
tale-swapping and private nightmares among high building iron-
workers (whose accidents are so bad as to deny them anything but
exhorbitant job-by-job insurance):

> [Patrick] *spent the first days showing me one thing after another.*
> *". . . The only thing you've got is the damned beam, and if I let go,*
> *or if you're heavier than I am so that my weight won't stop if from*
> *seesawing, you're gone. It's as simple as that! . . . And that's only*
> *one way. Harold Moustache went twelve floors onto the exhaust*
> *pipe of a diesel truck when his partner let a header bang into the*
> *empty column he was perched on. Shot him off like a catapult. An*
> *Indian kid I knew went off an apartment building when his part-*
> *ner let loose before he'd got a bolt stuck. The partner landed on*
> *the plank floor, but the kid slid off the end and over the side. . . ."*

> *Some nights, lying in bed after a day's work followed by one of*
> *Patrick's safety lectures, I'd have half-asleep fantasies of a faceless*
> *partner chuckling as he pushed a beam into my chest, knocking*
> *me over the side. Or of the weight ball banging into the column*
> *atop which I perched waiting for the header, making a terrible*
> *ringing noise that drowned out my falling screams.*

The writer, Mike Cherry, closes with the comment that such dreams
did not come often, as most of the time he loved the work — "But there
were nights like that."[23]

Since the passage in 1970 of the Occupational Safety and Health
Act (OSHA) some of the stress inherent in industrial accident and
toxic exposure has been relieved. Gains can be traced to employer
conformance with OSHA regulations, either to head off the bother of
a visit by one of 1,400 inspectors, a possible fine, or in unhappy
response to both. As well, many unions have used the Act's existence
to beef up their traditional workplace safety role in monitoring, grieving, and otherwise policing the more obvious and alarming of workplace hazards in the nation's 6 million workplaces.

Problems persist, of course, not the least of which is misrepresen-
tation of actual conditions when safety inspections occur. Typical is

the situation explained in this letter from a Machinist Union member to his union newspaper and its medical consultant:

> *Dear Dr. Mancuso . . . I filed a claim for loss of hearing due to my job. I am having a hard time because five of the other fellows who have been working with me also lost their hearing but are afraid to file a compensation claim or get some changes made on the job. When the company did noise measurements the foreman told all the workers not to turn the machines on while they are testing. Can a company do this?*

The doctor replied:

> *They can, but that doesn't make it right. This is the equivalent of fixing the records so that compensation claims can be denied with false data. The compensation officer judging your claim would not know that the company did this and wouldn't believe you even if you told him what happened.*

> *This is an important problem, because the basic question raised in compensation hearings is what the noise levels were over the previous years. Obviously you couldn't get an honest or accurate record from your place for the proper evaluation or support of your claim.*

> *What happened in your plant is not an isolated instance, but is also applicable to toxic chemicals throughout the country. Repeatedly I have been told by IAM [International Association of Machinists] members how a plant manager will curtail certain processes or stop using a certain chemical, or completely close down one or more operations, before an anticipated inspection by OSHA or some other investigator.*[24]

Blue-collarites I have known trade such stories from workplace to workplace, and keep them alive over many years as fuel for their muted, deep-bred hostility toward any who seem to put output ahead of human welfare . . . especially that of human beings like themselves.

Overall, then, the stresses where health and safety hazards are concerned remain varied and significant. To be sure, some substantial relief has been gained from the post-1978 vigilance of OSHA policy-makers and field inspectors. High jury compensation awards and climbing insurance premiums have goaded corporate prosafety measures, and labor union safety stewards and managers with conscience and/or productivity goals have turned their new-found OSHA-

Photo by Ken Light © 1979.

Machinist, Pan American Steel Co.: Workers are often faced with work situations that are not only dangerous but also poorly illuminated, making the work even more dangerous, tiring, and disspiriting.

backed authority to advantage. As well, the more constructive of media stories have probably helped, as in a "consciousness-raising" fashion, to spur safety concerns in and outside of the workplace.

On the other hand, however, the leading problem remains one that combines pressure for production with covert supervisory cover-up of related safety hazards. If an operator comes to believe that the only way he can make money on his piecework schedule is to feed material into his punch press at considerable risk to himself (as by placing his fingers occasionally between the dies), he will do so. And he will continue to do so if he has gotten away thusfar without harm *and* with increased production, especially if he also enjoys the toleration of a knowledgeable supervisor who boasts: "He is our best producer!"

WORK SETTING

The issue of "unpleasant working conditions" was the third rated work problem in the 1972-73 ISR national survey—and little wonder! While the settings vary widely from dockside to shed to highway, boiler room, and hangar, the same sorts of stressors are complained about across the board: The grievances here focus on "physical discomfort," "noise," "odors," "general neglect," and "the double standard."

The situation has undoubtedly improved since an outraged participant-observer argued in 1957 that the common absence of a single clean place to sit down in a factory was a revealing indicator of the low value that society placed on the factory hand.[25] But scattered and uneven improvements still leave considerable room for further improvement—as any time carefully spent in a wide variety of blue-collar work settings makes clear.

Part of the problem, of course, is native to the setting, as in outdoor work:

Ironworker: *The worst thing [about the weather] is the sheer physical discomfort. Hell, call it pain. Some people can take it better than others, but none of us is happy about it.*

. . . Any construction worker who tells you he doesn't hate [the cold weather] is either a madman or a liar.

. . . Winter! I began each day by listening to the weather report, praying to hear that the temperature was either over 25° or under 20° below. If it was in the twenties, I felt I could survive; at twenty below not even Mad Johnson, the foreman, could expect us to work.

. . . Whenever it got near a hundred, we knocked off, whether Crockett [the foreman] tried to shame us into staying or not. . . . Crockett stopped before us one day as we lay during a break sprawled on the ground like so many dogs in a Juarez street, put his hands on his hips, and snorted, "Jay-essus! In six months you'll be cryin' for weather like this. You'll be pissin' and moanin' and prayin' for good ol' summertime, just like you do every year, you memory-less bastards." [26]

Similarly, a bricklayer looks ahead to an accommodation—but of a different kind:

It can be brutal, especially in the winter. You can't work colder than 20 to 25 degrees because you can't wear gloves. The feeling of laying the brick is in your hand—you put a glove on and you lose it. My hands crack up. . . . When the temperature drops it can get bad, and you start looking forward to 32 degrees. When it's too cold you look for inside work. If there's nothing to do, you look for part-time jobs. I know a guy at a dating-bar and if it turns out like it looks right now, I'll work nights to pay the bills.[42]

Not surprisingly, then, college president John Coleman's greatest discomfort in 1973 as a "sabbatical-leave blue-collarite" was weather related:

It took only one half hour [of a day-long rain] . . . to soak [our garbage-collecting crew] to the skin. The denim pants and jacket I wore gave in to the rain first. Then, I felt the cold water penetrating my shirt and underwear. My feet soon squished in my boots and my hands squished in my gloves.[28]

"Along about then," Coleman notes, for the only time in his two-month experience as a blue-collarite, "I decided a college presidency wasn't such a bad job at all."[29]

Distress from job-based variations in temperature also occurs in a wide range of *indoor* settings, of course, and can be a daily trial: A seventeen-year-veteran meat cutter recently explained to me how he felt his frequent trips in and out of the freezer between counter sales in the supermarket had changed his very being:

You get used to it, you know. At first it was hard . . . I was chilled or frozen some of the time, and okay some of the time, and I couldn't control which of the times it was goin' to be [laughs]. . . . I've gotten used to it, and laugh at the new guys . . . at home, though, I've got to have the air conditioner on now all the time, and I do mean all the time. From spring 'til winter starts up again . . . I need that cool, all the time, or I roast . . . so I don't go out too much, like when it's warm. . . . I need that cool.

Blue-collarites employed in laundries, dry-cleaning plants, food-preparation kitchens, factories with a heat-dried paint component, warehouses with exposed platforms, and numerous other places spend eight or more hours daily on a temperature roller coaster without the associated fun.

Other stress components differ radically from come-with-the-territory aspects of the work setting, and many workers bitterly resent the double standard entailed:

"You know, they brag about this place," Penny said, "about all the windows, and what a nice view it has. Did you ever see a

*window down here? We don't have the view [in the factory]. The
offices have the view and we get to work with no windows."*

*The windows are just one of the discrepancies. Air conditioning,
just put into all the shops this winter, was in the offices long ago.*[30]

Similarly, workers note substantial disparities between their neglected
work stations and the pampered front office: in the noise quality level,
standards of cleanliness, general disorder, and even aesthetics (the use
of color, space, piped-in music, and so on). The double standard here
is taken by many as a stressful measure of calculated disdain, though
shrugged off by hard-boiled others who insist they are inured to "all
that dumb sort of thing."

Stressors in the work setting, then, are no puzzle or any subtle sort
of "closet matter." They are as plain as the factory windows that
haven't been cleaned for years, a toolshed floor that bears traces of
everything dropped on it in recent weeks, the odors from industrial
processes that inadequate venting never really removes, and the incessant cacophony of roaring, whirring, pounding, and whistling
noises that bring both lingering headaches and the risk of sustained
hearing loss. A litany of familiar grievances here extends to include
incessant air drafts, poor lighting, extreme temperature variations,
insufficient water fountains, second-rate lockers, poor maintenance of
plant bathrooms, and third-rate plant cafeteria settings (dull, depressing and debasing, to say nothing of third-rate institutional food or
coin-machine fare).

I have also listened to blue-collarites rail against the yearly re-
currence of unfilled potholes in the company parking lot. Or complain
about the slowness with which disabled pay phones and broken vend-
ing machines in the plant are repaired. Or dwell on the insulting
barrenness or banality of workplace decor (usually calendar art or dis-
carded posters). In general, the workers I have talked with have an
abiding suspicion that none of this really makes any difference to the
boss, that nobody "up top" really gives a damn about physical work
conditions down below (provided, that is, that workers have made
"the best of it," and that accident, turnover, and productivity levels
seem unaffected).

Newer factories, the current year's model in trailer-truck cabs, and
other such exercises in modernity are relatively free of many of the
stressors cited above, but do have some new problems of their own,
like design sterility and a hypermodernity that older workers find very

foreign. Their number remains miniscule, however, compared to the dominant versions nationwide of mean-spirited blue-collar work settings—and the related toll in stress reactions appears high.

WORK LOSS

Writing in 1932, during the Depression, Rex Hersey concluded that "of all the various forms of insecurity [earnings adequacy, accident risks, supervisory harassment, dismissal, etc.,] fear of unemployment proved most worrisome to all. . . ."[31] Today, the anxiety level here is similarly high, and the situation draws on a statistical base that blue-collarites can intuit even if exact numbers elude them; that is, blue-collar employment grew only 6 percent over the last five years, while white-collar employment increased 17 percent (clerical, 16 percent; professional and technical, 21 percent). Production worker totals in manufacturing dropped by 101,000, and the number of blue-collar semiskilled workers decreased by 38,000.[32] Little wonder, then, that as series editor Alan McLean puts it, "unemployment and the threat of job loss are exquisitely threatening to many; seriously disrupting to others."[33]

Blue-collarites have only their seniority to bolster their defense against layoffs, and that helps little when even a minor recession gets underway. Accordingly, every move by management is scrutinized for its possible impact on job security:

> Next to overtime grievances, the most vexing problem for a skilled committeeman or steward was outside contracting of work within a plant. It meant that every time a rigging company came into our shop to move a group of machines our crew lost that work and the probability of overtime. . . . The rage expressed over contracting of work is monumental.[34]

Some workers adopt self-endangering attitudes and behavior in their zealous pursuit of steady work, however much this might strike outsiders as a Faustian trap:

> Heavy equipment operator: We can't go out and get our own jobs. When we get laid off we have to call the union hall and they send you to a job whenever it's your turn. But there's so many people work for a contractor, say, for twelve, fifteen years, these people will do anything to keep their job. They don't think of the

safety of another operator, of his equipment or anything. They're doing things to please the contractor.[35]

Others seek relief from the anxiety of confronting layoffs through fantasies:

Many of the workers I met [in five months as a factory hand] know that the labor market for them is limited. However, they maintain the illusion of a different situation . . . [by] talking about someday leaving the shops. I heard workers with as little as six months' experience, and as much as twenty-five years, talk about leaving the company and taking other, more interesting, challenging jobs. Relatively few of them will leave. . . .[36]

Throughout blue-collar ranks, deep-reaching fear connects to the possibility of soon being separated from the payroll. Many dread separation thereby from *the* adult role that uniquely certifies acceptance by a powerful other (employer) and membership in the community of respectable peers (the gainfully employed mass of fellow beings). Many also know that working for a new employer, while welcomed for its affirmation of one's adulthood and value to others, means starting at the bottom again: Reemployed blue-collar males over forty-five, for example, will never qualify for the longer vacation period they had slowly worked up to in a previous job; this is no small loss for a household head who goes back to a rank beginner's two-week vacation schedule (and comparable cutbacks in retirement and insurance benefits).

Unemployment is its own special hell, regardless of what Sunday newspaper supplements suggest about the pleasures of subsidized idleness. Sociologist E. E. LeMasters offers five explanations:

1   The men resent the fact that it is not of their choosing, and thereby points up their lack of control over their fate.

2   They can get bored to the very edge of sanity.

3   They tend to drink more when they are not working. "Many of these men have what might be called 'a drinking problem,' which they control, at least in part, by not drinking on the job eight hours a day, five days a week. Unemployment upsets the delicate balance of their drinking program—partly because they spend more time at the tavern when they are not working."

4   Their marriages may become tense, as the wives are unaccustomed to having the husbands underfoot all day. "The husband, being upset by his inability to work, is not, of course, at his best in his marital role during this period."

5   The financial squeeze can be excruciating. Unemployment benefits help, but the gap between relief and earnings is very hard to accommodate—when the "fault" is not your own!

LeMasters notes, in conclusion, that "one of the best indicators of the importance of the job to these men is their discomfort when they can't work."[37]

REFORMS

What sort of comparatively new and promising reform notions here merit attention? While we must keep certain critical cautions clearly in mind (workplace skeptics initially doubt if reforms are worth the trouble, vested interests in the workplace defend the status quo, and so on), ten reform possibilities still seem well worth our review:

• Compensation stress *might* be alleviated somewhat if more workers were covered by *cost-of-living adjustments* (COLA). In the mid-1960s, only 2 million were covered, today, 5.6 million; roughly 60 percent of all union contracts contain COLA clauses (but 94 million other workers are still not covered). Designed to help protect workers' pay from inflation, COLA could work *against* inflation if the rise in prices can be slowed, for wage gains then could also be slowed in response.[38]

• Compensation stress *might* be lessened if more companies experimented with the *"cafeteria-style" compensation package plan*. This approach allows each worker to meet with a company compensation counselor, and design a custom-tailored formula for individual compensation benefits. Young singles, near-retirement oldsters, newly divorced or separated adults, new parents . . . all have wider options with which to meet personal needs and preferences. At present, employees may choose their own individual fringe benefits as a result of two little-noted sections of the 1978 tax bill: Employers can now provide minimal "core" coverage in life and health insurance, vacations, and pensions, while employees buy additional benefits to suit their own needs, using credits based on salary, service, and age.[39]

• Illness potential *might* be reduced by *prejob assignment screening* to cover genetic blood deficiencies and other sources of unusual sensitivity to industrial chemicals. To date, companies have focused on treatment *after* the fact; new gains can be had from a preemployment screening along with periodic employee monitoring.[40]

• Accident prevention *might* gain from a *joint labor-management educational campaign* to drive home such hard-nosed arguments as these three from the National Safety Council: If all work accidents could be eliminated and the cost savings distributed, every working person would receive a weekly raise of $4; a loss of productivity would be regained equivalent to the operation of all American industry for a full week; and, the savings would be equal to cutting the current 7 percent inflation rate by 25 percent.[41]

• Accident compensation *might* gain if workers began to keep *work diaries:* A safety specialist for the Machinists Union urges workers to "write down what happens at the work place. Write down every time any air sampling, testing or measurement of noise or toxic substances is done in your department. Record the date, the hour, the location of each test . . . (how many tests, and when), who conducted the tests, and what they were measuring. Write down the working conditions at the time, were they changed in any way before or during the testing and measurement? Also record what trade name products and chemicals and materials are used in your department."[42]

• Work loss dread *might* be lessened if other states followed California's example and began to *experiment with "partial" unemployment insurance.* In common practice, workers must be laid off all together before receiving jobless benefits. A new California law (spring 1978) permits an employer, with the consent of his workers, to share among the work force the reduced amount of work available rather than lay off individual workers. Employees become eligible for 20 percent benefits when put on four-day weeks, and this allows employers to cut hours worked. Employers can hold onto valuable people, full layoffs become unnecessary, and union dues continue to flow (the union must initially approve the cutback plan).[43]

• Work loss dread *might* be relieved somewhat by an *extension of supplemental unemployment benefits* (SUB) to the 90 percent of all employees in the private sector not now covered. First won by unions in the mid-1950s, SUB, in combination with unemployment insurance, pays incomes of up to 95 percent of after-tax wages to laid-off workers.[44]

• Work loss dread *might* respond favorably to a calculating requirement that *all entry-level job openings must be listed with the nation's fifty state employment service systems* (a similar requirement now applies to jobs under federal contractors, but is weakly enforced.)[45]

• Work loss dread *might* decline if labor, management, and government could agree on new legislation *to require advance notice from businesses closing or relocating.* One draft version of an Employee Protection and Community Stabilizing Act has four compenents: It would provide public loans and other financial assistance to keep companies from closing. It would require an employer to give a year's notice, wherever possible, to employees and the community. It would require an employer to offer suitable employment at the new plant or other plants operated by the employer; otherwise, an employer would give severance pay to each former employee now jobless. And finally, the proposed state legislation would require employers to make payments into a job development fund administered by the state Industrial Development Authority.[46] Another draft prepared by Senator Harrison A. Williams, Jr. (D-NJ) stipulates "adequate notice," rather than one-year prenotice, and champions employee stock ownership plans and federal loans to assist workers and towns in taking over viable enterprises as an alternative to plant closings.[47]

• Work loss dread *might* be alleviated somewhat if unions and companies experimented with incentives to *earlier retirement* and *shorter workweeks.* The United Auto Workers (UAW), for example, have won "30-and-out," or retirement with thirty years of service regardless of age, and 70 percent of eligible auto workers have retired since 1970 under this rule. The UAW has also won twenty holidays a year, which, combined with vacations, bring the workweek down to four and one-half days. Both of these contract gains try to slow the shrinkage in the work force, insulating older workers from unemployment and putting new workers on the job.[48]

Meant only as an illustrative, and by *no* means exhaustive list of relevant reform possibilities, these ten antistress options would seem to warrant open-minded and sensitive assessment by those managers, unionists, and workers who, in McLean's apt phrase, "can translate thoughts into constructive action." [49]

SUMMARY

Having deliberately sought out and focused on the four major objective work stressors that tax manual workers, I am left with a far-reaching list worth constructive response:

Blue Collar Work: Objective Stressors

Compensation	Inflation erodes purchasing power.
	"Cures" for inflation may spur unemployment.
	Workers feel they are being scapegoated for the inflationary spiral.
	Compensation has no assuredness of continuity.
	Sectors of the blue-collar work force vie with one another for economic advantage.
	Gains are secured by reliance on "category" rather than on individual merit.
Health and Safety Hazards	Use of inadequately tested components and processes leaves all uneasy.
	Fatalism, as a depressor of concern and prevention, asures uneven preventative measures.
	Pervasive anxiety haunts high-risk situations.
	Employer evasion of OSHA spirit and rules demoralizes employees.
	Industry opposition to spread of OSHA regulations casts industry in a cold light.
	Predominance of pressure for production encourages cynicism about employer motives.
	Media preoccupations with industrial hazards spread anxiety.
Work Setting	Physical discomfort (noise, odors, general neglect) is commonplace.
	Double standard in the care given to white-collar settings stirs jealousy.
	Out-of-doors exposure increases risk of illness.

Extreme variations in inside work conditions increases risk of illness.

Indifference to worker comfort (air drafts, dull walls, potholes in parking lots, etc.) deflates pride in employment.

Work Loss

Dread of layoffs pervades work life.

Anger at contracting work within a plant connects to intense inter-worker rivalries.

The experience of unemployment leaves all endlessly looking over their shoulder, fearing that job loss will catch them again.

Other items could be added, of course, but enough exists already to make a compelling case for *additional* remedial action: The parties directly involved (managers, unionists, workers) obviously accommodate these stressors daily, and are probably making incremental progress over time. But if I can trust off-the-record conversations, many would welcome an occasional fresh idea and a "shot in the arm" ... especially of the kind that results in expeditious moves and significant stress-reducing gains.

NOTES

1. Gary Gappert, *Post-Affluent America: The Social Economy of the Future* (New York: Franklin Watts, 1978), p. 47. See also Sidney Lens, "Disorganized Labor," *The Nation*, February 24, 1979, p. 208. In 1978 living costs rose 9 percent, the second biggest leap in thirty-one years, and real spendable earnings declined 3.4 percent. See "Real Wages Down 3.4 Percent for '78," *AFL-CIO News*, January 27, 1979, p. 1.

2. Ray West, Research and Education Director, Oil, Chemical, and Atomic Workers Union, as quoted in "Special Report: The Great Government Inflation Machine," *Business Week*, May 22, 1978, p. 136.

3. Marvin Friedman, "Where Have all the Flowers Gone?" *Viewpoint*, September 1, 1979, p. 14. See also Richard T. Curtin, *Income Equity Among U.S. Workers: The Bases and Consequences of Deprivation* (New York: Praeger, 1977).

4. As quoted in "Special Report," p. 119.

5. *Ibid.*, p. 117. From a report of the Council of Economic Advisors.

6. William W. Winpisinger, "Uphill All the Way," *Challenge*, March-April 1978, p. 44.

7. As quoted in *AFL-CIO News*, September 17, 1977, p. 1.

8. "Special Report," p. 136.

9. As quoted in Mike Cherry, *On High Steel: The Education of an Iron-worker* (New York: Ballantine Books, 1974), p. 69.

10. As quoted in Studs Terkel, *Working: People Talk About What They Do All Day And How They Feel About What They Do* (New York: Pantheon, 1974), p. 25.

11. John R. Coleman, *Blue-Collar Journal: A College President's Sabbatical* (Philadelphia: Lippincott, 1974), p. 187.

12. As quoted in Terkel, *Working*, p. 25.

13. As quoted in "Special Report," p. 136.

14. "Special Report," p. 117. From Joan Robinson's book, *Economic Heresies* (New York: Basic Books, 1971).

15. Richard Sennett and Jonathan Cobb, *The Hidden Injuries of Class* (New York: Vintage, 1973), p. 36. I rely heavily on this remarkable source in this discussion.

16. Franklin Wallick, *The American Worker: An Endangered Species* (New York: Ballantine, 1972), p. 5.

17. Hughes Rudd, *CBS News* (New York: May 10, 1977). All the statistics and the quotation from Senator Jacob Javits are from this report.

18. James O'Toole, ed., *Work in America* (Cambridge, MA: MIT Press, 1974), p. 26.

19. Steven Velman, "OSHA Under Fire," *The New Republic*, May 21, 1977, p. 20.

20. Coleman, *Blue-Collar Journal*, p. 172.

21. As quoted in a longer transcript in Kenneth Lasson, *The Workers: Portraits of Nine American Jobholders* (New York: Bantam, 1972), p. 65.

22. *Ibid.*, p. 147.

23. Cherry, *On High Steel*, p. 148.

24. From a column by Dr. Thomas Mancuso in *The Machinist*, August 1978, p. 2.

25. Harry Swados, "The Myth of the Happy Worker," in *A Radical's America* (Boston: Little, Brown, 1962), pp. 111-121.

26. As quoted in Cherry, *On High Steel*, pp. 88, 189-190.

27. As quoted in Lasson, *The Workers*, p. 157.

28. Coleman, *Blue-Collar Journal*, p. 241.

29. *Ibid.* See also Michael J. Colligan and William Stockton, "The Mystery of Assembly-Line Hysteria," *Psychology Today*, June 1978, pp. 93-94, 97-99, 113, 116.

30. Richard Balzer, *Clockwork: Life In and Outside an American Factory* (Garden City, NY: Doubleday, 1976), p. 142.

31. Rexford B. Hersey, *Workers' Emotions in Shop and Home: A Study of*

Individual Workers from the Psychological and Physiological Standpoint (Philadelphia: University of Pennsylvania Press, 1932), p. 381. See also Caroline Bird, *The Invisible Scar* (New York: McKay, 1966).

32. "Nation's Job Gains Over 5 Years Concentrated in Services, Trade," *AFL-CIO News*, January 27, 1979, p. 2.

33. Alan A. McLean, *Work Stress* (Reading, MA: Addison-Wesley, 1979), p. 55. See also Paul Jacobs, "A View from the Other Side: Unemployment as Part of Identity," in W.G. Bowen and F.H. Harbison, eds., *Unemployment in a Prosperous Economy* (Princeton: Industrial Relations Section, 1965), p. 9; Katherine H. Briar, *The Effect of Long-Term Unemployment on Workers and Their Families* (San Francisco: R&E Research Associates, 1978).

34. Bill Goode, "The Skilled Trades: Reflections," in B.J. Widick, ed., *Auto Work and Its Discontents* (Baltimore: Johns Hopkins University Press, 1976), p. 36.

35. As quoted in Terkel, *Working*, p. 25.

36. Balzer, *Clockwork*, p. 143.

37. E.E. LeMasters, *Blue-Collar Aristocrats: Life-Styles at a Working-Class Tavern* (Madison, WI: University of Wisconsin Press, 1975), p. 26. All of the quotations are from this page. See also Coleman, *Blue-Collar Journal*, pp. 94-111; McLean, *Work Stress*, pp. 47-56.

38. Jerry Flint, "Cost-of-Living Adjustments Create Difficulties in Controlling Inflation," *New York Times*, August 1, 1978, p. A-10.

39. See in this connection Edward D. Lawler, "Workers Can Set Their Own Wages—Responsibly," *Psychology Today*, February 1977, pp. 109-110. See also "Companies Offer Benefits Cafeteria-Style," *Business Week*, November 13, 1978, pp. 116, 121. Unions insist that employees receive adequate counseling, preferably by both company and union, and that the overall cost of the benefit package remains the same as it would be under conventional coverage.

40. Gail Bronson, "Industry Focuses on 'Hypersusceptible' Workers; Prove Allergies, Other Maladies Caused on Job," *Wall Street Journal*, March 23, 1978, p. 46.

41. "Accident Economic Drain Affects All Facets of Life," *Pittsburgh Press*, January 16, 1979, p. A-10. The article quotes Vincent L. Tofany, president of the National Safety Council.

42. Thomas A. Mancuso, "Help for the Working Wounded," *The Machinist*, August 1978, p. 2.

43. "Labor Letter," *Wall Street Journal*, August 15, 1978, p. 1. See also Betty Yarmon, "Work-Sharing Plan Can Pay Off for You," *Pittsburgh Press*, April 3, 1979, p. A-12.

44. James S. Henry, "The New Conservative Theories of Unemployment," *Working Papers*, March-April 1979, p. 77.

45. *Ibid.*

46. Acel Moore, "Law Urged to Require Companies about to Close to Give Notification," *Philadelphia Inquirer*, February 19, 1979, p. 2-B.

47. "Capital Wrapup," *Business Week*, February 19, 1979, p. 117.

48. "UAW Fears Automation Again," *Business Week*, March 26, 1979, p. 95. UAW President Douglas A. Fraser contends that the four-day week is "absolutely inevitable. The only open question is how fast we're going to get there."

49. McLean, *Work Stress*, p. ix.

READING:
AUTOMATION, LABOR, AND
CONSTRUCTIVE ANSWERS . . . NOW!

Technological displacement is a constant hazard in blue-collar employ, and this stressor outdistances almost every other in taking a toll of worker equanimity. Helpful in illuminating one especially constructive type of blue-collar response is this thoughtful and frank essay from Kenneth W. Yunger, a former student of mine at the AFL-CIO's George Meany Labor Studies Center.

We are living in a rapidly automating, highly technological age. Many men have sung the praises of automation; many men have reviled against the acceleration of technology. My concern is the effect of automation on the middle-class workingman and his family life. I base this concern and analysis on current experiences in my present workplace. I base it also on my personal feelings since I am one who has been automated out of work previously and will be automated out of work again in the near future.

The circumstances surrounding my automated unemployment began taking shape three years ago. At that time I was a printer spending most of my working day setting type for a newspaper. I was automated out of that job as well, and in an effort to keep me (and two other printers) working with the same employer, I was offered a job in the newspaper's mailroom. Since the mailroom job entailed a cut of only six dollars per week in salary and afforded an opportunity to refresh some little-used skills and an opportunity to learn some new ones, I took the job. The other two printers also accepted. This transfer involved management's cooperation, unusual intra-union cooperation, and, with little encouragement, the individuals' cooperation.

An explanation of the "unusual intra-union cooperation" is necessary to this extent: the printers and mailers in my shop are in the same international union but have separate local unions (an arrangement that is basically illogical and advantageous to neither party). In past years, the two have occasionally been at odds with one another and I'm sure that the arranged transfer of printers to the mailroom was accomplished with great difficulty. I'm not familiar with the circumstances of my transfer prior to its actually occurring, but there surely was some resistance to the transfer on the part of the membership of the mailers' union for the very simple reason that three more employees in the mailroom meant fifteen less shifts of overtime for the current mailer membership.

The circumstances that afforded me the opportunity to work in the mailroom are not pertinent to this paper, although their analysis would make an interesting case study. Suffice it to say that inter- and intra-union cooperation in transferring employees, especially in the face of quickly advancing technology, is a first step toward reducing unemployment trauma in the publishing industry.

The point is eventually reached when *all* departments feel the touch of automation, and it is this point which concerns me now. During the last three years, management has pressed the mailers' union to provide more and more help to reduce overtime. This was accomplished by the transfer mentioned above, by bringing in mailers from other cities, and by training three apprentices—a total of twelve men were added to the original crew of thirty-five. The other nine men were added after much management-union discussion over how to eliminate overtime in the mailroom. Suggestions were made from the union's side that management should consider automation. This was done with the thought in our minds that they *were* considering automation, and that if we glutted our mailroom with help and then management *did* automate, we would face a large unemployment problem. Needless to say, one year after putting on the last nine men, the employer purchased the equipment which now causes the twelve most recently employed men to face the realities of unemployment.

Most of us have learned to live with being automated out of a job. The three ex-printers have experienced it before. They and six of the mailers know they can find work in other towns. My greatest concern is the three men who have only worked in the trade for one or two years, may not wish to travel, and face limited job choices in this geographical area. If they want to remain in a union shop, they have *no* job choice in the area since the shop we are in now is the only one under contract. How can we limit their trauma when faced with the loss of a good job? If it is their first job, how can we assure that they will be able to fit into other types of work, especially since this is the only shop in the area in which they can use their present skills? Keeping all twelve men in mind, what are the responsibilities of the union and the company toward these men, especially when both parties knew that their positions would likely be only temporary?

Concerning the temporary aspect of the jobs, it was management's responsibility to so inform the union that the help the employer begged for would only be working temporarily. If these twelve men, and especially the three apprentices, had known this when they took the jobs, they could have made a logical judgment at that time as to whether it was worth it for them to go ahead and train for a job they may only hold for two years. In the absence of this approach, and in the interest of alleviating their present lack of work, the employer, as a chain newspaper owner, should at least allow these men the opportunity to work at one of their other newspapers in the area, *regardless of their past experience*. If these men have the basic abilities to engage in any type of work, it is the employer's responsibility to train these men for other types of newspaper work. If they can learn to be mailers, they can learn to be pressmen, cameramen, even reporters or salesmen. Employees seldom cross the nonproduction-production line in the industry. The employer should make a substantial effort to encourage this crossing so that vacancies within his newspaper plants can be filled by workers who he is automating out of work.

The stability of a worker's family hinges on his opportunities for finding and keeping work. The worker who is in a position of not knowing whether he will be able to work enough days in a given week to support his family will reflect this instability in his home life. The instability increases when the days worked from week to week vary greatly. With only short notice (twenty-four hours) of what a man will work in a given week, it becomes difficult for him to plan any nonwork activities with his family. This becomes even more traumatic when, in order to get his five days for the week, a worker must work two shifts within twenty-four hours once or twice a week. A situation like this has to undermine durable family relations. The family unit is weakened by the lack of parental presence, especially if the worker's spouse also works. In securing a worker a job which can assure him fixed days worked each week and an adequate income, the employer would go a long way in reducing the trauma presented by the threat of loss of a job and the varying work hours caused by partial unemployment.

The employer must consider the effects of "automation unemployment" on human emotions and the worker's family. He can eliminate much adversity from the partially unemployed worker by making other job offers at early stages of automation. Early frankness with the union and employees that automation will reduce the number of jobs available, and tendering of replacement jobs and on-the-job training for those employees affected can only help enhance the employees' attitude toward their employer. It will also help reduce the trauma attendant to the usual job-losing and job-finding process.

This process of providing jobs for workers losing them to automation could be extended to an interemployer operation. Arrangements could be made with employers within a geographical area to cooperate with each other in making job referrals regardless of worker experience. As long as the employers agree on realistic basic requirements for workers and further agree to train the workers on the job, much of the impact of automation could be eliminated. The final extension of this training concept would be to provide workers off-the-job specialized training that would be used in their new job. The employers must keep in mind the savings realized in welfare and unemployment insurance costs and even the savings in affected human emotion and family instability that would derive from cooperation of this type. These things considered, it would pay for employers to bear the cost of training workers on the job.

The unions involved in dealing with automation have no less responsibility than employers in blunting the impact of this inevitable process on individuals' jobs. Intraunion processes already exist for informing employees where jobs are abundant or scarce. The traditional journeyman's card enables these workers to travel from one town to another without needing special qualifications in order to obtain a job. They need only show their card and pass a basic competency test in order to start a new job in a different city.

Interunion cooperation could be established within a given geographical area to allow workers to cross from one trade to another. Periodical notices could be interchanged between different unions to keep each other current on job openings that cannot be filled otherwise. Like employers, the unions should agree to realistic basic qualifications that job candidates can meet in order to be considered for a job opening. From this point the employer can assume responsibility for further training to fit the worker into the job. Opening of the communication lines between the unions is most crucial. If jobs go begging in a particular industry covered by union contracts, it certainly is to the union's benefit to find union workers, even from different industries, to fill those jobs.

Automation and technology acceleration will no doubt be with us for years to come. The suggestions above will be adequate for the near future. As jobs are automated out of existence, others are automated into existence. Thus is the need for on-the-job *re*-training also established. Workers automated out of jobs should have first option on retraining for newly created jobs. Especially when the process occurs within the walls of a given employer. Assuming fewer jobs are created than are eliminated, the suggestions I have given can alleviate some of the job-loss shock created by automation. When, and if, automation reaches the point where jobs are simply eliminated and none are created, we will have to consider changing much more than the means of obtaining and keeping jobs. We will have to change our whole concept of society and work.

Kenneth W. Yunger is secretary-treasurer of Topeka Mailers' Union No. 55 (Kansas). Born in 1947, he worked in a weekly newspaper production from 1965 to 1972, when he switched to the newspaper company room and first joined a labor union. Active as a union officer since 1976, he helps negotiate contracts, organize new workers, and conduct union education programs. Married and the father of a daughter, Ken fills "all [his] extra time" with union business.

2

BLUE-COLLAR WORK: SUBJECTIVE FACTORS

Alarmists aside, and conceding room for debate, there appears to be a general consensus on all sides that work in our society is not as economically effective, nor as pleasant and rewarding, nor as safe and secure as it ought to be, and this sentiment has arisen despite substantial objective advances in pay, benefits, and physical working conditions.

STANLEY E. SEASHORE*

All of us are sensitive to the opinion others have of our work, and if we conclude that people we respect do not place an especially high value on it, we are inclined to wince and worry. Similarly, we all want fair and respectful supervision. Erratic and oppressive bosses demoralize and infuriate us, even if the situation compels our (deceptive) acquiescence. Many of us especially value the camaraderie and support we enjoy from coworkers, but when cliques and rifts set all against all, the dues can be very high. Finally, we expect a modicum of satisfaction from our work, nothing out of the ordinary or unrealistic, but enough to enable us to privately believe that the good outweighs

---

* "Social Change and the Design of Work Organizations," in T. H. Hammer and S. B. Bacharach, eds., *Reward Systems and Power Distribution* (Ithaca, NY: ILR Publications Division, N.Y.S. School of Industrial and Labor Relations, Cornell University, 1975), p. 6.

the bad, and that the deal we've struck (as represented both by our line of work in general, and our own job in particular) isn't so bad after all.[1]

These four subjective aspects of work—*status, supervision, sociability*, and *satisfaction*—entail especially costly stressors in the lives of America's white male blue-collarites. Their stress reactions, and a small number of potential reforms, are reviewed at length below to help round out the analysis of workplace realities that I began in the preceding chapter.

STATUS

Leaving aside the unemployed (discussed later), blue-collarites occupy the bottom rungs of this nation's occupational status ladder. To be sure, the social standing of blue-collar work, or the honor or social esteem in which it is held, varies from high for craftsmen (tool and die makers, locomotive engineers, master electricians or plumbers, power station operators) to quite low for unskilled workers (ditch diggers, ushers, waiters, shoeshine "boys"). Overall, however, the general public apparently thinks little of manual work when it comes to measuring its standing according to the five dimensions Americans use in assessing a job—money, power, prestige, nature of the work, and amount of job prerequisites (such as necessary schooling). Blue-collar work in general comes off poorly—and blue-collarites generally know it.

This, of course, is the rub of the matter. In a mass culture like ours, with television, movies, and magazines zealously reinforcing selected stereotypes, the low status of blue-collar work appears to be commonly recognized both inside and outside the working class. Some token effort *is* made to alter or even reverse the situation with the holding of annual Labor Day ceremonies, union skills displays at county fairs and in shopping center plazas, and so on. Weak and sporadic, these public relations gestures pale in comparison to the task: In a society where prestige largely hinges on exclusivity (graduate or professional school diplomas), evidence of the ability to initiate action for others (the authority to give more orders than one takes), and the markings of work-linked sophistication ("brainwork," clean work, self-paced work, etc.), the competition in status assignment is stacked against blue-collarites from the start.

Stress follows when a worker takes to heart the low opinion

others hold of his livelihood—and such vulnerability may be common in the ranks. Typical is this revealing reply John Coleman, a participant-observer researcher, received when he asked a coworker, a ditch-digger, how the hiring of casual laborers operated:

Simple. It's about the same way they buy and sell cows. You get there about five-thirty or six in the morning and sit on one of their bare benches until a call comes. The guy who runs in says, "O.K., you—and you—and you." He crowds the gangs for two or three jobs into the back of an old panel truck—no windows, no heat. Then some young punk drives us out to the jobs, drops us off, gets a receipt for us, and disappears. If he's any good, he finds out when to pick us up again. If he isn't, we just wait. We do what we're told for the day. Then it's back into the truck, except it smells more by then, and back to the hiring hall. We get paid each night—and if we're smart we get drunk right after. Same thing the next day. You never know what you'll be doing. And nobody gives a shit anyway.[2]

Similarly, Coleman found many restaurant dishwashers "resigned to the fact that they are near outcasts: 'We're the scum of the earth and there's always somebody around to remind us of it.' "[3]

Blue-collarites with whom I have discussed this cultivate many different defenses against those who look down on them. Some disguise their job title, as did a gravedigger Studs Terkel interviewed who explained: "I usually tell 'em I'm a caretaker. I don't think the name sounds as bad."[4] Some shut themselves off psychologically from the work role: certain garbage collectors Coleman came to know "simply close up into themselves once they are on the route, get the job done, and get out of those neighborhoods as fast as they can."[5]

On the contrary, other blue-collarites find the best defense is an offensive posture. These workers make much, in a status-boosting way, of the critical character of their jobs:

Garbage collector: I don't have any regrets. I'm not complaining. There are better jobs around, and I'm not all that crazy about this one with the grind and the hustling and the smell, but I don't think of it as the lowest of the low. Somebody's got to do it. Can you imagine what it would be like if nobody wanted to pick up garbage?[6]

Garbage collector: Frankly, I'm proud. I'm doing an essential task, like a policeman or a fireman. I left this country a little cleaner than I found it this morning. Not many people can say that tonight.[7]

Gravedigger: *Not anybody can be a gravedigger. You can dig a hole anyway they come. A gravedigger, you have to make a neat job. I had a fella once, he wanted to see a grave. He was a fella that digged sewers. He was impressed when he seen me diggin' this grave—how square and how perfect it was. A human body is goin' into this grave. That's why you need skill when you're gonna dig a grave.*[8]

Steam fitter: *I'm proud of what I've done with my life. I come from humble origins, and I never even finished school; but I've gotten someplace. I work hard, but it's good work. It's challenging and never routine. When I finish a day's work, I know I've accomplished something. I'm damned good at what I do, too. Even the boss knows it.*[9]

Pride in craft, pride in self—these stress-combatting strengths exist and persist in the ranks, but only as the prized possessions of a minority who value them in large part for their covert and highly private nature.

Some men stand out in possessing esoteric and refined skills: Mike Cherry, a former math teacher who became an ironworker, offers a fine illustration of coworker strengths:

I've known men who worry every payday because they are afraid they are being cheated. They can't reassure themselves because they can't add up the columns of deductions, or if they make the attempt, come up with the wrong answer and an earful of ballpoint pen ink. Yet they can suggest a dozen or more ways to make a recalcitrant piece of iron go where it's supposed to, ways that would simply not occur to a new man, even if he held a Ph.D. from M.I.T.[10]

A variation here stresses skill gains achieved over time. Labor leaders lend their voices—and celebrity status—to promoting this theme:

George Meany: *The difference in the requirement for a skilled worker today and when I was an apprentice and a young journeyman—there just can't be any comparison. . . . For the installations now . . . you've got to have highly skilled mechanics, and the quality of the work has to constantly improve.*[11]

Similarly, electricians take pride in pointing out that their work has become so complex that their union (International Brotherhood of Electrical Workers, AFL-CIO) has recently been employing more than fifty-seven members for the task of constantly revising textbooks used in the union's job-upgrading courses.[12]

Photo by Ken Light © 1979.

Iron Worker, High Steel: This iron worker, decked out with his equipment, perches himself dangerously as a regular part of his job. He is proud of his work and skill, his bravado a key element in his manhood.

Some of this pride-in-craft, however, is being steadily undermined by certain technological "advances"—part of the perpetual battle in which workers try to maintain their prestige as skilled workers, while various employers and engineers try to build that same skill into machine processes.

Other workers, in a defensive reaction to their own low occupational status, rely instead on a macho-based denigration of "them," the anti-blue collar world of higher-status white-collarites. Many I have listened to on this topic argue that their "sweat labor" is a damn sight more honest, more manly, more honorable than a lifetime spent "shuffling papers" or earning a living "with your mouth." (Sociologist E.E. LeMasters, judging this smugness "*the* major problem in the attitude of these men toward work," worries that it is "not very helpful in a society that is becoming increasingly white-collar") (italics added).[13]

In this same vein, a powerful prostatus device involves steadfast insistence that the "little people" possess superior wisdom and sounder political positions in current controversies over gun control, lenient judges, and so on:

> Garbage collector: *The way I was brought up, right is right and wrong is wrong. Some got an education and some don't, but the people that have a little common sense can still tell you what's right and what's not right.*[14]

These two blustering forms of smugness—"our work is realer than yours!" and "our morality is sounder!"—falter somewhat under challenge, and are therefore generally retained in a low-keyed and relatively private way, one that protects them from close scrutiny or challenge.

When blue-collarites occasionally speculate about the sources of their low status they *can* be unsparing of themselves—and revealing of *much* buried stress: A 37-year-old steel mill laborer, for example, offered Terkel this commentary:

> *I'm a dying breed. A laborer. Strictly muscle work . . . pick it up, put it down, pick it up, put it down. We handle between forty and fifty thousand pounds of steel a day. (Laughs) I know this is hard to believe—from four hundred pounds to three and four-pound pieces. It's dying . . . . You're doing this manual labor and you know that technology can do it.*[15]

Self-denigration becomes an unexceptional part of the scene:

Old hands never tire of telling new men that the only two pre-requisites of the iron-working trade are a size eighteen shirt and a size three hat.[16]

Pipefitters in self-denigration refer to the necessary attributes of their trade as "a strong back and a weak mind."[17]

Still another reason for the low state of dignity in auto plants may be the belief prevalent among workers that jobs on the line do not require "brain work"; or as the common saying in auto plants goes, "You need a strong back and a weak mind to work here."[18]

Low status, then, finally edges out almost every possible antidote—save one of a time-honored nature: the abandonment of interest in work in favor of interest in the things work can help one consume. Troubled by the conviction that society insists on undervaluing their work, blue-collarites seek status and prestige, instead, from the fact that their inflation-driven earnings are "more than the old man ever brought home," this a flimsy dodge most finally recognize as inadequate to beat their own "low-status blues."

SUPERVISION

Two major subjective stresses that blue-collarites associate with super-vision involve the enervating pettiness of various work rules and the enervating nature of relentless pressure for more and more produc-tion.

Work rules

While the situation varies widely, many and perhaps most blue-collar work settings are laced through with "dos and don'ts" that resemble nothing so much as the regulations of primary school, Sunday school, or boot camp. There are rules about where to park, when to arrive, when to eat, how often to use the bathroom, where to smoke, when to smoke, whether or not to smoke, whether or not to talk with co-workers, whether or not to stretch or stroll a bit, when to wash up before the day's end, when to line up at the time clock, how fast to move on the way out, and so on and so forth. Prohibitions against chewing gum, and currently fervid campaigns against smoking—some going so far as to actually make it grounds for dismissal—are part of workplace lore in this exasperating and nerve-touching matter.

Considerable aggravation stems from widespread rank-and-file recognition that no other segment of the nation's workforce has its day so closely regulated and policed as do blue-collar workers. Typical is this blue-collarite's report:

> It's the hypocrisy that gets to you, the double standard. They try to sell you this crap about how you're important, and then you find it's only the people in the shop who have to punch in and punch out. We can't smoke, we can't do this or that, but they can.[19]

The double standard, here as elsewhere in blue-collar life, galls beyond exaggeration and is a mental stressor never far from the surface.

Not surprisingly, a conspiracy of rule violators serves as a strategic stress reducer and solid boost to employee solidarity. This conspiracy of coworkers helps adult employees demonstrate to themselves, and also to significant others, that they can *still* express some personal control over the work environment: A participant-observer notes that

> . . . smoking in the bathroom has evolved into something more than simply breaking a rule. The worker has found . . . a place that has not been designated by the company. Since a worker often feels that much if not all of what he does is done in places designated by the company, under company control, finding ways to express personal freedom from this institutional regimentation is important.[20]

When one's workday is as structured by others as it is for many tightly regulated manual workers, "being able to do something illegal can become very satisfying."[21]

So long as the company winks at the reasonable bending or violation of its official rules—as in ignoring bathroom "nicotine addicts" —much stress is avoided. Crackdowns, however, violate previous understandings or implicit "contracts" assuring specific forms of permissiveness. At these times pent-up outrage triggered by a crackdown can take the form of understandable retaliation that includes:

- Spreading rumors and gossip to cause trouble at work
- Doing work badly or incorrectly
- Stealing merchandise, supplies, or equipment
- Damaging the employer's property, equipment, or product accidentally, but not reporting it
- Damaging the employer's property, equipment, or product on purpose.[22]

In explanation, one assembly line worker has characterized sabotage as "just a way of letting off steam":

> You can't keep up with the car so you scratch it on the way past. I once saw a hillbilly drop an ignition key down the gas tank. Last week I watched a guy light a glove and lock it in the trunk. We all waited to see how far down the line they'd discover it.[23]

Pressed for reasons, the now-angry worker retorted, "Look how they call us in weekends, hold us extra, send us home early, give us layoffs. You'd think we were machines the way they turn us on and off."[24]

Certain work rules, in short, can gall more than they goad, and exasperate those loudly reminded of them by new or overzealous supervisors. Workers, of course, have many different explanations of the boss's need for "law and order," only few of which promote better employer-employee relations. Almost regardless, however, how they finally view the employer's case for work rules, many blue-collarites feel diminished by the robot-like obediance the rules would compel.[25]

Production pressure

As if to deliberately make things harder, the work world of blue-collarites also includes an incessant expectation of greater production, however unreasonable that may nominally seem:

> To expect a production worker to work at his peak for a whole day is like asking a long-distance runner to sprint the whole race the way he does in the last 100 yards.[26]

Business Week, seemingly impressed by this logic, has recently urged its readers to recognize that characteristic blue-collar responses to relentless pressure for production are "very human and not really much different from that of mnagers who want to gain freedom and autonomy on their jobs."[27]

Sociologist Bill Goode, who previously spent a decade as an auto plant pipefitter and UAW committeeman, contends that "there never has been a job, regardless of the skill of engineering, that workers have not been able to improve upon and shorten the operating time."[28] When occasionally aware of this, management may strain to take advantage and—more often than not—blunders badly. Blue-collarites learn to resist top-down attempts to increase production because their experience has taught that the reward for higher turnout is primarily a renewed demand for still greater output, *ad infinitum*.

Techniques for "keeping the heat on" are many and varied, though most, as forms of harassment, entail ways of pressuring a person or keeping him in a corner. Certain supervisors about whom I have heard colorful stories provoke, frighten, browbeat, intimidate, or in other related ways push productivity goals—and not incidentally, stir considerable (debilitating) stress. A method of delivering an object lesson, this sort of harassment is popular with managers who need to demonstrate their dominance, or to indicate indifference about whether any particular worker stays or quits, or to keep subordinates tense or anxious.[29]

Blue-collarites, to be sure, are generally inured against a *conventional* amount and style of supervisory harassment (young workers are taught by old hands that "it's easier to shit downward than upward," meaning that one must expect and accept a certain amount of injustice from above). But, beyond a point which varies subtly with an individual's personality, acceptable harassment can turn into conflictual and intolerable stress:

> *Some of the actual causes . . . are those created by new managers, by excessive emphasis on production, by disregard of the needs of the workers, by the tediousness of the task involved and resultant boredom, by lack of management appreciation of extra effort and application, and by the effects of the aging process that the workers have not recognized.*[30]

Linked to Douglas McGregor's infamous Theory X, a hard-driving style of supervision currently discouraged in college and MBA courses in personnel relations, harassment earns blue-collar responses (retaliation, low morale, sabotage) far afield from its overt goal of getting the work out.

Reprinted by permission of the Chicago-Tribune New York News Syndicate, Inc.

Work rules and production pressures, in short, are exceedingly sensitive tools in the supervision of human beings. If they are to reward, they require a deft hand and considerable maturity in application. Supervisors are hard pressed to convert attendant stresses into desired production; far too many unhappily earn, instead, covert sabotage, bizzare outcomes, and a pervasive guerilla war at work between "us" and "them."

SOCIABILITY

To remain comfortable as one of the crowd while enjoying acceptance by "significant others" among one's coworkers is perhaps *the* highest-order workplace need of the largest number of employees. Indeed, blue-collarites I have discussed this with explain that the second biggest job reward, next only to wages and fringes, is the kidding around, the fun and friendship you can enjoy with the gang at work. This leeway to "schmooze" with the guys (that is, to do things unrelated to their assigned work) is regarded by many manual workers as an absolutely indispensable prerogative of workingmen (and women).[31]

Blue-collarites heavily invest in work group affiliations, especially as adult counterparts of yesteryear's valued teen-age gang or warmly remembered neighborhood "corner boy" group. (Asked to explain their practice of going together, twenty men strong, to successfully protest the firing of another worker a sawmill group explained: ". . . we work together, we drink together, we play poker together, we lie to our wives together. So we got some practice sticking together."[32]) Where social affiliation needs are comfortably met, a worker has the security of coworkers' support, camaraderie, and an invaluable source of tips on "where influence lies, where respect is deserved, and where support is forthcoming."[33]

In a lighter but no less significant vein, a group member can also enjoy raw-boned antics that draw on humor to help pass the time:

> *An assembly line always has artifacts for involved horseplay: tubing, metal washers, bolts, empty kegs, all provide the materials for elaborate gags. This play is largely slapstick, never subtle, and often with more than a touch of malice. A handful of washers on a steel floor will tip over a cart that a worker sits on to wheel himself under a car body. Tubing and cold water provide great, if not delicate, possibilities for humor.*[34]

Critical in such horseplay is prior assurance that all will be taken in the right way and that no bad feelings will erupt or linger after. The gang is expected to see the joke and appreciate not only its humor but also its help both with passing the time and reaffirming bonds of human solidarity.

Distress enters, however, when the common need to be part of a community at work is thwarted by sharp-edged divisiveness. Men endlessly succumb to the temptation to arbitrarily exclude, isolate, and denigrate certain of their own coworkers. In the aftermath of such internecine warfare, work force harmony is replaced by numerous cliques that may divide blue-collarites by age, sex, race, lifestyle, religion, educational attainment, region, ethnic origin, marital status, political attitudes, leisure preferences, standards of morality, or occupational attitudes and aspirations . . . and so on and so forth.

Typical are these comments on the criteria used to rationalize stress-inflating divisiveness among coworkers:

Nightshift auto worker: " [*Angry at overachievers*] *It's the hill-billies . . . . The union calls them to a meeting, says, 'Now don't you sabotage, but don't you run. Don't do more than you do.' And everybody cheers. But in a few days it's back to where it was. Hillbillies working so fast they ain't got time to scratch their balls . . . .*"

I ask who he means by the hillbillies. "Hillbillies is the general (local) term for assholes, except if you happen to be a hillbilly. Then you say 'Polack.' Fact is everybody is a hillbilly out here except me and two other guys. And they must work day shift 'cause I never see them."[35]

Ironworker: [*Recalling hazing directed at new men*] *On the climb the pusher asked me if it was my first job, and I nodded that it was. He made a face that would have gone nicely with the discovery that his girlfriend had syphilis, but said nothing. I wondered what had made him ask the question, not knowing then that new men and old hands don't even walk the same way.*[36]

Spot-welder: *Oh sure, there's tension here. It's not always obvious but the whites stay with the whites and coloreds stay with the coloreds . . . . When two men don't socialize, that means two guys are gonna do more work, know what I mean?*[37]

Heavy-equipment operator: *Oh yeah, every union has a clique. I don't care what union it is, their own people are going to work*

> *more. I mean their brothers and their son and such like that . . . .*
> *Sure, there's a lot of colored boys do real good work. You set*
> *down with 'em and you have your lunch and there's no hard*
> *feelings. But there again, they hate you because you are some-*
> *thing. You didn't get this just through a friend. You got it through*
> *hard work and that's the only way you're gonna get it. I was an*
> *apprentice and I worked my way out.*[38]

Add to this the time-honored workplace rivalries between the Masons
and the Knights of Columbus, the gentiles and the Jews, the hippies
and the straights, and several other such costly demarcations . . . and
the American blue-collar version of traditional Balkan guerilla warfare should be clear.

Since the government's 1964 campaign began to insure affirmative
action on behalf of women and nonwhite minorities, the stress possibilities in work group solidarity have soared:

> *Amid all the general racial antagonism that existed, what people*
> *seemed to resent most bitterly (in a 10,000-person plant) was what*
> *they considered the company's bending over backward for min-*
> *orities.*[39]

White blue-collarites seethe with rumors that not only are minority
applicants given preference in hiring, but that they also later enjoy
special treatment when promotions are being weighed.

Bitter resentment against the double standard plays a large part in
keeping white blue-collarities opposed to "affirmative action." An
unemployed veteran ironworker offered this analysis in 1971 to coworker Mike Cherry:

> *Commie clerks and longhairs and school teachers and Johnson-*
> *ites—t'ey don't know shit. But t'at don't keep 'em from buttin' in.*
> *"Here, now," t'ey say. "Take t'is here poor black bastard into your*
> *union and let him get some of t'at wonderful money you're*
> *makin'. He's starvin' to deat' and runnin' up t'e welfare rolls." So*
> *you say, "Why don't you take him into your business? Let him be*
> *a big banker, or a school principal, or somet'in."*

> *"Oh, well," t'ey say, "we couldn't do t'at. He's uneducated, you*
> *see, so he wouldn't fit in wit' our kind. But you guys are all*
> *dumbhead dropouts anyhow, and he'll fit in wit' you just fine.*
> *Besides, you know you're way overpaid for just plain old manual*
> *labor, and you ought to share the pie."*[40]

By way of ending his analysis, the older worker exploded with this one-sentence explanation of the whole thing: "Shit! I'm not prejudiced; I'm just tryin' to make a livin'!"[41]

Women are the newest target for this resentment, as this factory work angrily contends:

> They've got a new slavery in here. It's the white man who's the slave now. In here if you're white, and especially if you're a man, you might as well forget about getting ahead.[42]

Tensions here are likely to remain high for several years ahead as Supreme Court developments alter the white male's hegemony over prized blue-collar posts. Blue-collar males insist it is not "dumb prejudice" they feel so much as outrage over being *told* whom they must accept as workplace peers. And despite the assurances that company and union officials offer, the "boys of the shop floor" remain very bitter toward minorities receiving what they perceive as supports white males did not enjoy and still cannot call their own.

Workpace sociability "ain't what it used to be," as a once-homogeneous white male preserve is forced to give way to overwhelming prochange pressures from the government. White male blue-collarities struggle to protect their self-interest against *all* claimants, especially those they perceive both as threatening a system that has paid off (in white male privileges) and as asserting "superiority" over them: White male blue-collarites grimly fear that gains by women and non-whites could just prove to be their loss.[43]

Blue-collar camaraderie today appears to be a source of demoralizing strains that mix hostility with patronizing compassion:

> The men pity the women because they do the slighter tasks.
>
> The women think it's all right for them but pity a man who has this for his career.
>
> The blacks pity any white who'd have to take a job like that.
>
> The whites pity the blacks who won't ever get anything better.
>
> The young people feel sorry for the old people who can't move on.
>
> The old people feel sorry for the young people who are so unsettled.[44]

Social acceptance goals persist, of course, and the need for companionship here will last so long as humans, and not robots, are punching time clocks. These goals and needs are not being fulfilled, however, in the clique-ridden world of many antagonistic blue-collarites.

SATISFACTION

The picture of satisfaction with work has revealing and complex contradictions: Poll data, for example, suggest many workers are "satisfied" with their work, but interview data uncover much work-related discontent. Blue-collarites tell me, for example, that they would never do it all over again, and many are intent on seeing to it that their children do *not* follow in their footsteps. ("Not so bad," a common response to survey questions here, often means the worker has no hope of soon getting anything better or cannot immediately recall any blockbuster grievance to relate—and so, shrugs the who thing off.)

Helpful here are the thoughts of Irving Bluestone, a UAW vice-president who helps lead the quality of worklife campaign in union circles. He scoffs at the survey data that suggest workers like their work:

> . . . there is little else the worker can say. What are his alternatives? He has a job; it's a stinking job: it's a repetitious and monotonous job. It bores him to death—he has to be always thinking of something else while he is working or he'll go crazy. But also, he has to accommodate himself to it because that job is the only way he can earn a living and support his family. There is no point in knocking what one has to do, even for a survey questionnaire.[45]

Similarly, a thirty-seven-year-old steel mill laborer explained his reluctance to get in touch with his real feelings about his work:

> My attitude is that I don't get excited about my job. I do my work but I don't say whoopee-do. The day I get excited about my job is the day I go to a head shrinker. How are you gonna get excited about pullin' steel? How are you gonna get excited when you're tired and want to sit down? . . . Unless a guy's a nut, he never thinks about work or talks about it. Maybe about baseball or about getting drunk the other night or he got laid or he didn't get laid. I'd say one out of a hundred will actually get excited about work.[46]

Overall, then, the characteristic blue-collar response to the challenge of finding satisfaction in work entails reducing one's goals so far that one can appear to be satisfied.

Where stressors are concerned, work satisfaction is compromised by a large number of deterrents, including some that are commonly overlooked, such as busywork (the empty tasks assigned only to fill time until regular work is again available.) Workers I have known commonly resent the operating premise here that "idle hands mean mischief." Many are embittered by this childish practice:

> *The following day of busywork was nearly unbearable. . . . I told one of the women how insulting I had found it and how much it had upset me.*

> *"Now you know how it feels," she said. "It is insulting. Almost all of us who have worked here know that feeling. It's degrading to know that you're being given work just to keep your hands busy. It's hard to feel that you're important when you know that. They let you know that you are expendable. They let you know that no chair and no job is yours. They move you around at will. That's why workers feel unimportant."[47]*

Not surprisingly, a worker's common stress-reducing response to busywork, or to highly routinized labor, is to go on "automatic pilot," or turn off his or her mind to help the time pass. (A forty-one-year-old garbage truck driver with eighteen years seniority explained to Terkel: "You get just like the milkman's horse, all he had to do was whistle and shooshh! That's it. He know just where to stop, didn't he?"[48])

Helpful in grasping the full range and variety of major antisatisfaction stressors is a new report from researchers on the attributes of those with and without "blue-collar blues," that is, a cluster of negative job attributes such as low morale, alienation, discontent, and so on:

High "Blues" Level	*Low "Blues" Level*
Had some skills they would like to use on their jobs but can't.	Skills were fully used on the job.
Had little chance on their job to learn new things.	Received enough help to do their work best.
	Had enough tools, machinery, or other equipment to work their best.
Received few fringe benefits.	Received many fringe benefits.

Had a supervisor who did not hold to high performance standards in his or her own work.

Had a supervisor who left his or her subordinates alone unless they wanted help.

Photo by Earl Dotter; reprinted with permission.

The entire 8-hour shift every day, day in and day out, is spent putting wheel rims on a conveyor belt, week in and week out, month after month, and often year after year.

As the researchers judge their own results "the message is clear: The Blue Collar Blues are predominantly associated with those working conditions that discourage good work performance, impede personal growth, and stifle autonomy and creativity. Having relatively poor fringe benefits is also important."[49] Assembly line workers, followed closely by the occupants of other tedious blue-collar jobs, report the greatest boredom and job dissatisfaction. As well, they also have the highest levels of anxiety, depression, irritation, and psychosomatic disorders.[50]

Discontent is especially prominent among younger blue-collar workers. Many begin with individualistic notions and a belief in the value of work in and of itself. But in short order they are disillusioned, "definitely feel more exploited than older groups, and desire participation in decision-making."[51] A recent study of white male blue-collarites in Baltimore and Detroit found the same differences by age group:

> The older our respondents, the more satisfied they were, both with their living standards and with their job, irrespective of income level. Age seems to be a proxy for realism. The options of the young become the constraints of the old, and they are perceived that way. Unattainable goals are abandoned or modified as time passes.[52]

Similarly, the study of the "blue-collar blues" referred to earlier concludes that it is not those between thirty and fifty years of age, but younger men who are inordinately subject to this social malady.[53]

To be sure, some of this dissatisfaction is applauded by scholars as evidence of a healthy refusal to accept blind obedience or to surrender complete control to the "system." Dr. Robert Reiff, a former auto worker who is currently a psychiatrist, sees this as evidence that many

Reprinted by permission of the Chicago Tribune-New York News Syndicate, Inc.

blue-collarites "feel angry at being exploited, resentful at being mistreated, and frustrated at the limited control they do have. It is because they feel *human* (rather than like defeated robots or interchangeable mechanical parts) that they have these feelings."[54] At the same time, however, all of this and even higher levels of absenteeism, lateness, restiveness, turnover, and grievance filing, along with low levels of morale and productivity, make a case for the sort of reform response we turn to below.

REFORMS

Under active field-test review now, or likely to be so in the near future, are thirteen or so reform proposals especially worth judicious and imaginative attention:

• Work status *might* profit from workplace forms of *acknowledging blue-collar contributions*. A thirty-seven-year-old steel mill laborer explained his idea this way to Studs Terkel: "I would like to see on one side of (every tall building) a foot-wide strip from top to bottom with the name of every bricklayer, the name of every electrician, with all the names. So when a guy walked by, he could take his son and say, 'See, that's me over there on the forty-fifth floor. I put the steel beam in.' Picasso can point to a painting. What can I point to? A writer can point to a book. Everybody should have something to point to."[55]

• Work status *might* profit from more *work enrichment experiments* modeled on the UAW-Harmon Co. (Bolivar, Tenn.) project. Six years ago, the union and management created a network of more than thirty shop-floor committees. So successful were they at raising morale and productivity that workers gained free time while at work to attend their own remarkable school, the only one of its kind inside factory walls. Courses, which included hydraulics, leadership skills, ethnic cooking, black culture, and car care for women, were taught by workers, managers, and regular instructors. Particular pride was taken in the fact that this ego-boosting program had been designed from the bottom up, and was "not one designed by concerned managers with the help of social scientists and imposed on the plant."[56] (A 1977 study of 180 joint committees, while conceding the obstacle here as the traditional mistrust between labor and management, forecasts a "continuing but gradual increase in the number of cases of cooperation."[57]

• Work supervision *might* profit from experiments with popular new approaches like *transactional analysis*: "At General Motors Fisher

Body Plant No. 2 in Michigan, union representatives and managers took a weekend course in transactional analysis, so they could understand how to deal better with employees. 'I see supervisors treating people better,' a UAW representative says. 'Instead of saying, "Hey, you go over there and sew," they say, "I sure would appreciate it if you'd help out over there." ' The new climate, she says, 'makes things far more satisfying for the employees.' "[58]

• Work sociability *might* profit from experiments with *behavior modeling*, a new training technique used by over 300 major companies in the late 1970s. Similar to sensitivity training in that it tries to preserve an employee's self-esteem, it differs in that it attempts to teach participants to deal with specific problems. Specialized programs have helped smooth relations between coworkers whose jobs could create conflicts. Blue-collarites at Exxon's Baytown, Texas, refinery, for example, have learned how to deal with a coworker not doing his or her job, respond to peer pressure, handle a complaining coworker, or show appreciation to a coworker. While the entire concept is still undergoing fine tuning, it is already "clearly creating an improved atmosphere. . ."[59]

• Work sociability *might* profit from *affirmative action programs* that actually offer new opportunities to all, rather than to only some blue-collarites; for example, Robert F. Young, the Director of Urban Affairs for New York Telephone Company, reports that their Upgrade and Transfer Plan, which enables nonmanagement employees to file written requests for better jobs, "has been used successfully [since 1973] by over 16,000 employees. I am sure that this has had a positive effect on morale."[60] Similarly, Xerox Corporation has created a human resource planning program which is computerized; an employee's history and expected levels of attainment are recorded, and as positions become available, the computer identifies qualified candidates and advancement interviews are invited.[61]

• Work satisfaction *might* profit from workplace experiments with *flextime* (except for a fixed core of hours during the middle of an eight-hour shift, employees can arrive and leave at will, provided they work the required number of hours per week and complete their assignments on time). Flextime is based on the assumption that employees should be able to choose their own hours, within reason, rather than work a fixed period determined arbitrarily by the employer or by tradition. Flextime thus offers blue-collarites the autonomy and flexibility customarily enjoyed only by managers and professionals.

"Flextime treats employees like responsible adults rather than children to be watched. . . . The idea that such trust is possible in the organizations of modern industrial civilization may well be flextime's greatest contribution."[63]

• Work satisfaction *might* profit from a *fresh assessment* of a reform once hailed as the wave of the future, but now vulnerable to the question of whether it has any future at all. This reform, *the compressed work week* (four days, forty hours), is opposed by certain labor unions and there are problems with restrictive overtime laws and employers' schedules of worktime. Despite much hoopla and expressions of favorable support on its mid-1970s introduction, the Labor Department believes only 2 percent of all workers are presently on the job fewer than five days a week.[64] At the same time, however, the rise in the use of national holidays that fall on Monday has nearly all of American industry operating on a four-day workweek for 15 percent of the year—and leisure commentators remain confident that rearranging nonwork time into useful blocks of three days (and more) *is* a solidly based trend (although it may take the form of the UAW auto industry pattern, whereby individuals take off separately and the production process goes on continuously).

• Work satisfaction *might* profit from company experiments with a popular personnel tool, *sensing sessions*. In these sessions, executives sit down with employees to frankly discuss, face to face, what is on the minds of the rank and file: "Some [sessions] involve meals, while others are held in conference rooms. Some companies choose attendees randomly—every sixth name on an alphabetized list of all employees, for example,—while others group participants by job category, length of service, or the like. Some use consultants or managers from different divisions to run the meetings, while at others the top managers go it alone with their people. The method seems immaterial—the bottom line for all of them is, at the least, an across-the-board boost in morale."[65]

• Work satisfaction *might* profit from *experiments with employee access to their own personnel files*. Typical here is a law enacted in Pennsylvania in November 1978, reflecting a "growing belief among workers nationwide that unless they have access to their records, their progress or standing with a company might be damaged by incorrect or misleading information." The Pennsylvania law permits a worker to see information about salary, overtime, employer evaluations, disciplinary actions, commendations, and similar matters. At the same time, the law prevents a worker from seeing letters of recommendation written on his or her behalf, records pertaining to allegations of criminal conduct, and medical records. As well, the law permits only one inspection of the file a year, and in this way prevents harassment of employers by excessive review requests.[66] A similar law, enacted in Michigan on January 1, 1979, also requires employee notification if disciplinary reports are sent outside the corporation.[67]

• Work satisfaction *might* profit from experimentation with the idea of *work modules*, the smallest allocation of time that is economically and psychologically meaningful. If the work of a spot-welder, for example, is construed as consisting of four 2-hour modules, he or she might spend two at welding, one at testing new equipment, and another at a drill press operation that he or she enjoys as a change of pace. All such choices, of course, would be consistent with the operating constraints of the company. And if no one chooses "unattractive" work modules, workers would be assigned according to seniority or some such criteria. Naturally, any union on the scene would have to be heavily involved. Among its other possible benefits, the work module approach should lead to increased job satisfaction and better self-utilization (use of one's skills and abilities) and self-development (acquisition of new skills and abilities). Likely to relieve bordom and enrich work life, the module concept would help workers gain invaluable discretion in crafting work lives of their own design.[68]

• Work satisfaction *might* profit from experiments with the *New Economic Process (NEP)*. Hailed by labor and management for shifting emphasis from conflict to cooperation, NEP committees in the workplace attempt to design new product lines, upgrade skills, lay out plants more efficiently, cut waste, and share gains from increased productivity. Born of necessity in conflict-weary Jamestown, New York, the NEP approach is very careful to respect existing collective bargaining arrangements by staying out of wages, hours, vacations, overtime, or other traditional labor contract issues. Jamestown's mayor, Stanley L. Lundine, now a congressman, has urged Congress to pass legislation he has introduced supporting NEP experiments across the country.[69]

Other reforms could be cited, of course, as with well-known antistress success in using job rotation, internal plant transfers and promotion opportunities, job enrichment or restructuring designs, or employing autonomous work groups of the Scanlon Plan.[70]

Whatever the specifics, those who weigh the case for reforms concerned with *subjective* aspects of blue-collar work should consider the heart of the matter: A local union president explains that he and his friends "simply [want to have] something to say about what *we're* going to do. We just want to be treated with dignity. That's not asking a hell of a lot."[71]

SUMMARY

Where are we heading in the matter of status, supervision, sociability, and satisfaction? Are things any better or worse now than in recent years past? And should we take comfort or alarm from the trends we can discern? While much variation naturally exists across the blue-collar scene, a dominant pattern of subjective work experience *may* course through contemporary workplace reality. For example, judging from the material gathered nationwide from 1969 to 1977 by the University of Michigan Survey Research Center, job satisfaction has declined markedly in the past eight years, and fewer workers feel their jobs are useful, relevant to future productivity, or equal to their skills:

> *The decrease was about equally distributed among five areas—comfort, challenge, financial rewards, resource adequacy, and pro-motions—but was absent for the sixth, relations with coworkers.
> ... Men reported greater declines in satisfaction between 1969 and 1977 than did women. ... The decline was virtually identical for white and black workers. ... Workers in the higher skilled occupations (professional, technical, and managerial jobs) exhibited a smaller decline than did those in lower skilled occupations (operatives and laborers).*[72]

In all then, the subjective side of the blue-collar stress picture would seem to merit *all* the constructive reform attention possible—from without, but especially from within the world of work.

I wasn't particularly surprised by the negative things I saw in factories: speed, heat, humiliation, monotony. ... It was the positive things I saw that touched me the most. Not that people are beaten down (which they are) but that they almost always pop up. Not that people are bored (which they are) but the ways they find to make it interesting. Not that people hate their work (which they do) but that even so, they try to make something out of it.

... workers make a constant effort, sometimes creative, sometimes pathetic, sometimes violent, to put meaning and dignity back into their daily activity.

Barbara Garson, *All the Livelong Day: The Meaning and Demeaning of Routine Work* (New York: Penguin Books, 1975), p. xiii.

NOTES

1. See in this connection Ogden Tanner, *et al.*, *Stress* (Alexandria, VA: Time-Life Books, 1976), pp. 82-83, 91; Ruth M. Walsh and Stanley J. Birkin, eds., *Job Satisfaction and Motivation: An Annotated Bibliography* (Westport, CT: Greenwood Press, 1979).

2. As quoted in John R. Coleman, *Blue-Collar Journal: A College President's Sabbatical* (Philadephia: Lippincott, 1974), p. 28.

3. *Ibid.*, p. 162.

4. As quoted in Studs Terkel, *Working People Talk About What They Do All Day and How They Feel About What They Do* (New York: Pantheon, 1974), p. 508.

5. Coleman, *Blue-Collar Journal*, p. 242.

6. As quoted in Kenneth Lasson, *The Workers: Portraits of Nine American Jobholders* (New York: Bantam, 1971), p. 30.

7. As quoted in Coleman, *Blue-Collar Journal*, p. 224-225.

8. As quoted in Terkel, *Working*, p. 507.

9. As quoted in Lillian R. Rubin, *Worlds of Pain: Life in the Workingclass Family* (New York: Basic Books, 1976), p. 156.

10. Mike Cherry, *On High Steel: The Education of an Ironworker* (New York: Ballantine, 1974), p. 108.

11. As quoted in an interview by Nick Kotz, *New York Times*, September 4, 1977.

12. William L. Abbott, "Beating Unemployment Through Education," *The Futurist*, August 1978, p. 215.

13. E.E. LeMasters, *Blue-Collar Aristocrats: Life-Styles at a Working-Class Tavern* (Madison, WI: University of Wisconsin Press, 1975), p. 25.

14. As quoted in Lasson, *The Workers*, p. 23.

15. As quoted in Terkel, *Working*, p. 4.

16. Cherry, *On High Steel*, p. 21.

17. Bill Goode, "The Skilled Trades: Reflections," in B.J. Widick, ed., *Auto Work and Its Discontents* (Baltimore: Johns Hopkins University Press, 1976), p. 40.

18. Al Nash, "Job Satisfaction: A Critique," in Widick, ed., *Auto Work*, p. 67.

19. As quoted in Richard Balzer, *Clockwork: Life In and Outside an American Factory* (Garden City, NY: Doubleday, 1976), p. 142.

20. *Ibid.*, p. 90.

21. *Ibid.* For striking parallels with the attitudes, behavior, and plight of young "delinquents," see Richard Sennett and Jonathan Cobb, *The Hidden Injuries of Class* (New York: Vintage, 1973), pp. 79-90.

22. Robert P. Quinn, "Evaluating Working Conditions in America: Is the Sky Really Falling?" in Robert P. Quinn and Linda J. Shepard, *The 1972-73 Quality of Employment Survey* (Ann Arbor: ISR, 1974), pp. 259-260. In this entire paragraph I draw on this article.

23. As quoted in Barbara Garson, *All the Livelong Day: The Meaning and Demeaning of Routine Work* (New York: Penguin, 1975), p. 93.

24. *Ibid.*

25. Outstanding here are two new accounts from the workplace: Charles Spencer, *Blue Collar: An Internal Examination of the Workplace* (Chicago: Lakeside Charter, 1977); Richard M. Pfeffer, *Working for Capitalism* (New York: Columbia University Press, 1979).

26. Garson, *All the Livelong Day*, p. 215.

27. As quoted in John Hoerr, "An Insider's View of the World of Work," *Business Week*, July 10, 1978, p. 12. (Book review, Robert Schrank, *Ten Thousand Working Days*, Cambridge, MA: MIT Press, 1978.)

28. Goode, "The Skilled Trades," p. 36.

29. Carroll M. Brodsky, *The Harassed Worker* (Lexington, MA: Lexington Books, 1976). I draw here on a rare study and excellent source. See also Joseph F. Follman, Jr., *Helping the Troubled Employee* (New York: American Management Association, 1978).

30. As quoted in Ivar Berg, *et al.*, *Managers and Work Reform: A Limited Engagement* (New York: Free Press, 1978), p. 27. "Conflict" served here as a euphemism for antiunionism, and this manipulative orientation continues to haunt the subject.

31. For unique insights into workplace "schmoozing," see Schrank, *Ten Thousand Working Days* (see note 27).

32. Garson, *All the Livelong Day*, p. 112.

33. Jon Miller and L.J. Fry, "Work-Related Consequences of Influence, Respect, and Solidarity in Two Law Enforcement Agencies," *Sociology of Work and Occupations*, November 1977, p. 472.

34. As quoted in Goode, "The Skilled Trades," p. 39.

35. As quoted in Garson, *All the Livelong Day*, p. 93.

36. As quoted in Cherry, *On High Steel*, p. 21.

37. As quoted in Terkel, *Working*, p. 160.

38. *Ibid.*, p. 26.

39. As quoted in Balzer, *Clockwork*, pp. 268-269.

40. As quoted in Cherry, *On High Steel*, p. 68.

41. *Ibid.*, p. 69.

42. *Ibid.*,

43. Especially helpful in this regard is David T. Wellman, *Portraits of White Racism* (New York: Cambridge University Press, 1977), pp. 74-107, 216-236. "Racism . . . need not be distinct, in its content or emotional loading, from the more routine forms of competitive behavior white people engage in with other whites" (p. 236).

44. Garson, *All the Livelong Day*, p. 20.

45. Irving Bluestone, "Work Humanization in Practice: What Can Labor Do?" in W.J. Heisler and John W. Houck, eds., *A Matter of Dignity:*

Inquiries into the Humanization of Work (Notre Dame, IN: University of Notre Dame Press, 1977), p. 175.

46. As quoted in Terkel, *Working*, pp. 2, 5.

47. As quoted in Balzer, *Clockwork*, p. 141.

48. As quoted in Terkel, *Working*, p. 147.

49. Stanley Seashore and J. Thad Barnowe, "Demographic and Job Factors Associated with the 'Blue Collar Blues,' " in Quinn and Shepard, eds., *The 1972-73 Quality of Employment Survey*, p. 549.

50. Robert D. Caplan, *et al.*, *Job Demands and Worker Health: Main Effects and Occupational Differences* (Washington, DC: NIOSH Research Report, Government Printing Office, 1975).

51. Rogene A. Buchholz, "An Empirical Study of Contemporary Beliefs About Work in American Society," *Journal of Applied Psychology* 63 (1978): 225.

52. Burkhard Strumpel, ed., *Economic Means for Human Needs: Social Indicators of Well-Being and Discontent* (Ann Arbor, MI: Institute for Social Research, 1978), p. 154.

53. Seashore and Barnowe, "Demographic and Job Factors," p. 537.

54. Robert Reiff, "Alienation and Dehumanization?" in Widick, ed., *Auto Work*, p. 48.

55. As quoted in Terkel, *Working*, p. 2.

56. Daniel Zwerdling, "Workplace Democracy: A Strategy for Survival," *The Progressive*, August 1978, p. 18. Cf. James Rovins, "Costly Problem," *Wall Street Journal*, March 14, 1979, pp. 1, 35.

57. William L. Batt, Jr., and Edgar Weinber, "Labor-Management Cooperation Today," *Harvard Business Review* 56 (January/February 1978): 96-104.

58. *Ibid.*

59. "Management: Imitating Models: A New Management Tool," *Business Week*, May 8, 1978, p. 120.

60. Robert F. Young, "Affirmative Action Under a Constant Degree," *ILR Report*, Spring 1979, p. 24.

61. Robert J. Landsman, "Ho Do You Start to Move People into the Higher Levels of Management During a Time When the Economy Is Constricting and Opportunities Are Diminishing?" *ILR Report*, Spring 1979, p. 25.

62. "The Hardships That Blue-Collar Women Face," *Business Week*, August 14, 1978, p. 40.

63. Barry Stein, Allan Cohen, and Herman Gadon, "Flextime: Work When You Want To," *Psychology Today*, June 1976, p. 80. See also "Part VI, Flexible Working Hours," in Thomas G. Cummings and Edmond S. Molloy, *Improving Productivity and the Quality of Work Life* (New York: Praeger, 1977) pp. 205-234.

64. "Labor Letter," *Wall Street Journal*, July 25, 1978, p. 1. See also David M. Maklan, *The Four-Day Workweek: Blue Collar Adjustment to a Non-*

conventional Arrangement of Work and Leisure Time (New York: Praeger, 1977).

65. "Deep Sensing: A Pipeline to Employee Morale," *Business Week*, January 29, 1979, p. 124.

66. "Workers Gain Access to Their Personnel Files," *Philadelphia Inquirer*, November 19, 1978, p. 3-B.

67. George Corsetti, "New Law Aims at Spying on Employees," *In These Times*, November 8-14, 1978, p. 7.

68. See in this connection Robert L. Kahn, "The Work Module—A Tonic for Lunchpail Lassitude," *Psychology Today*, February 1973, pp. 35-39, 94, 95.

69. Michael Sterne, "Upstaters Try New Theory of Capital-Labor Relations," *New York Times*, August 16, 1976, p. 28. For a powerful critique of all such approaches see Richard Sennett, "The Boss's New Clothes," *New York Review of Books*, February 22, 1979, pp. 42-46. See also Richard Edwards, *Contested Terrain: The Transformation of the Workplace in the Twentieth Century* (New York: Basic Books, 1979); Ivar Berg, *et al.*, *Managers and Work Reform* (see note 32).

70. Excellent in this connection is Cummings and Molloy, *Improving Productivity* (see note 63); Louise E. Davis and Albert B. Cherns, eds., *The Quality of Working Life: Problems, Prospects, and the State of the Art*, vol. 1 (New York: Free Press, 1975); Raymond A. Katzell, *et al.*, *A Guide to Worker Productivity Experiments in the United States, 1971-75* (New York: New York University Press). For a highly rated practical guidebook for participatory management, see Fred Rudge, *The Key to Increased Productivity: A Manual for Line Executives* (Washington, DC: BNA, 1977).

71. Terkel, *Working*, p. 193.

72. Graham L. Staines and Robert P. Quinn, "American Workers Evaluate the Quality of Their Jobs," *Monthly Labor Review*, January 1979, p. 4. See also "Job Satisfaction Has Decreased, Study Shows," *ISR Newsletter*, Spring 1979, pp. 10-11. A revealing small-scale case study of value is Alice Heasley Dwight, "Once a Blue-Collar Worker, Always a Blue-Collar Worker?" *The Vocational Guidance Quarterly* 26 (June 1978): 318-325. Her Baltimore area data have her ask: "What will be the consequences if approximately 75 percent of the blue-collar workers in industrial areas of large cities are dissatisfied?" See also Barbara A. Gutek, "Satisfaction Guaranteed: What Does It Mean?" *Social Policy*, September/October 1978, pp. 56-60. For a dismaying case study that calls for reforms, see Gregory Giebel, "Corporate Structure Technology and the Printing Industry," *Labor Studies Journal* 3 (Winter 1979): 228-251; Carl Torgoff, "Comments," *Labor Studies Journal* 3 (Winter 1979): 253.

3

BLUE-COLLAR LABOR UNIONS: SHOP-LEVEL ISSUES

For me the union has been good. You have to remember the Depression. When we were kids, anybody who had a job was supposed to be really great. That's what life was. It's an idea that really sticks with you. And, with the Teamsters, I've had a good secure job. I've made more money than I ever dreamed of. If I get sick, they'll pay for it, and if I die the wife will get something. Those are the things you can't laugh at. The Teamsters have given this to me.

AL BARKETT*

Steelworker Charles Spencer recently culminated twenty-five years of work in a Chicago steel plant with the writing of a remarkable book, *Blue Collar: An Internal Examination of the Workplace.* In this book he divides his attention among his coworkers ("plain, obscure, everyday blue collar workers for whom work is the only choice"), his bosses ("not the Chamber of Commerce or the Harvard School of Business rendition, but, rather, the authentic management people in the hierarchy of the workplace"), his workplace ("where the blue collar workers spend the greatest part of their lives"), and his experience with labor unions ("their internal procedures, their agreements and disputes with their employers, their agreements and disputes with their own mem-

---

* Al Barkett, a $28,000-a-year over-the-road trucker, as quoted in Steven Brill, *The Teamsters* (New York: Simon & Schuster, 1978), p. 287.

bers, their patterns of collective bargaining, their role in restraining the workers").

"Does collective bargaining really work?" Spencer asks. "Are unions in bed with the companies? Are they in firm control of their members? How many miles and moons is it from the international headquarters in Washington and Pittsburgh to the workplaces in South Chicago and Detroit?"[1]

Spencer's questions, and many related others, connect to the fact that few aspects of the workplace reality of blue-collarites are as strategic, and yet as poorly understood by outsiders as those connected with the local union; its distant progenitor, the international union; their national spokesman, the AFL-CIO; and their collective symbolic representation, the American Labor Movement.

While barely a fourth of all workers are present dues payers, the vast majority of traditional blue-collarites (in contrast to those in the newer service work occupations) *are* labor union members: The importance of shared governance (shop stewards and foremen), the "rule" of labor contract terms, and the reassurance available to them in the threat of an ever-ready collective response (slowdown, wildcat, authorized strike) cannot be exaggerated, even though detractors may readily misrepresent the situation.

Significant here are local union politics, dissident struggles to unseat incumbents, local union support services, and other colorful aspects of the shop floor world that commonly elude media and outside attention. While much of this helps to relieve stress and make life far more bearable at work, some of this undoubtedly exacerbates tension and taxes workers in many telling ways. Local union meetings regularly end with a "Good and Welfare" free-for-all that crackles with such stress-focused excitement:

> The time was largely spent in members airing grievances against management, in protests against union action and/or inaction, and in educating the rest of us from workers' own personal experiences on such matters of common concern as health hazards and discrimination within the plant. This was the exciting part of the meeting . . . the time that a sense of worker collectivity emerged . . . when workers talked about what they needed and deserved. This was a time for anger and joy.[3]

The sources of both the anger and joy, the stress and relief, as they are connected to the blue-collarite's relationship with his local union, are what I explore below in some detail.

The local union

To begin with, this union level is the most significant to the average rank-and-filer; it encompasses the nation's 56,000 shop-place locals, which are a fascinating amalgam of protest agent, mediation aid (between employees and supervisors), productivity guide (both in pegging and also in prodding output levels), "theater company" (for acting out personalities of key agents), and "settlement house" aid (as in the ventilation and remediation of vexing personal problems).

Pivotal, of course, in all of these local union services are the officers—the locals' presidents, secretaries, trustees, grievance committeemen, stewards, and other functionaries:

> Most rank-and-file members have little contact with higher union officials; the individual who represents them in their grievances with management, keeps them informed of union activities, and listens to their complaints is the union.[3]

Everything is reduced to a straightforward set of relations, as explained by a no-nonsense international union president:

> Most of the members don't know who the hell I am. Most don't go to union meetings. If they're mad at the foreman, the company is no good; if they're mad at the union steward, the union is no good.[4]

Especially, then, in their roles as shop stewards, many local unionists relieve stress by policing and enforcing the workplace contract: Savvy foremen commonly consult with such unionists before making any move they suspect capable of stirring rank-and-file discontent. Similarly, dues payers take comfort in the notion that they can turn to their steward for "due process" protection whenever a management representative takes an action which the worker feels is unfair, unwise, unsafe, or in some other way unacceptable.

While the rule of the contract requires that a contested action be executed, albeit under protest, the later filing of a grievance and the arduous "grieving" of the incident up through channels is a hard-won prerogative that helps keep *all* work-related parties in line. (Grievances protesting discipline constitute "the overwhelming majority of complaints of blue-collar workers . . . [and] are most usually settled in favor of the company before they are processed."[5])

Five particular local union stress relievers *and* stress inducers especially warrant our attention, and each—*managing conflict, managing collaboration, managing heartache, managing elections,* and *managing dissent*—are examined below in order to set the stage for several reform possibilities both labor *and* business might find intriguing.

MANAGING CONFLICT

Shop stewards and local union officers are expected by rank-and-filers to orchestrate just the right amount of workplace militancy. A subtle formula here calls for just enough of the "hang tough" approach to keep up morale, but not so much as to stir unnecessary trouble. A former UAW shop steward, for example, has written recently of the stress-relieving ingenuity local unionists must exercise:

> . . . *we were caught in a bind: if we told the workers not to do the job, we could be penalized for violating the collective-bargaining agreement; if the workers refused to do the job, they could be penalized for insubordination. . . . Of course, some stewards, including myself, would sometimes go out on a limb and encourage a carefully managed slowdown, making it appear to be the voluntary action of the workers themselves.*[6]

Everything here must remain disguised, as a steward who gives the impression of being a hothead or "having a bug up his ass" is quickly unpopular: Workers that I have known commonly want *less* stress at work, *not more*, and will oust misguided, supercharged, antiemployer, militant stewards. Critics may condemn this unionist (and coworker) as an irresponsible radical, an overly ambitious politician, or an irrational sorehead, all grounds serious enough to help ensure later ballot-box defeat.

At the same time, however, stewards are expected to see faster, deeper, and farther than any ordinary dues payer, and to make waves when that seems grimly necessary. A local union health and safety coordinator, for example, was among the first to miss old work buddies and wonder where they were going:

> *I found that there are a number of people that I knew personally that I did not see around anymore. Going through the death certificates, I was appalled at the number of the cancer deaths at my one plant.*[7]

Immediately after, this unionist helped form a statewide committee on occupational safety and health, and had his local hire the services

Photo by Earl Dotter; reprinted with permission.

Such daily exposure has led as many as 85,000 workers to suffer from "brown-lung" disease, another of many health hazards shop stewards monitor daily.

of a leading university researcher, and began the local's campaign to win specific reforms in the plant ("We're not trying to close the plant, but to see if we can clean it up if it's found to be harmful"[8]).

MANAGING COLLABORATION

In the matter of steering a course between the temptation to conflict and the preferability of peace, attention should be directed to labor's role as an indispensable permission giver. Employers eager to gain the cooperation of workers with major changes in work rules can ask local union leaders for help, as when Boeing-Vertol sought to switch some blue-collar employees from military to nonmilitary production processes:

> [The conversion] would not have been accomplished without concessions by U.A.W. Local 1069. But the prospect of continued employment assured labor's cooperation. The union agreed to modified seniority and other work rules for the transfer of workers from helicopter production into roughly comparable classes of work in the rapid-transit field. Retraining was mainly done "on the job."[9]

In other circumstances, a local union leader may take the heat himself, as in making a tough decision that nobody welcomes but everybody concedes must be made. For example, a consultant to failing companies recalls:

> ... I recently became involved in restructuring an older New England plant employing 600 people which is no longer competitive. The union president stated, "I want to save jobs for this region. In order to make any of the jobs in this plant secure, I recognize that we will have to figure out how to operate this plant with 500 or even 400 employees."[10]

Note his use of the pronoun "we": the unionist apparently recognizes the need in such situations to share responsibility with those whom he might not collaborate with otherwise.

One way or another, however, "permission slips" negotiated by local unions with particular employers remain a strategic option labor has in the struggle to smooth things out, to ensure job survival, and to considerably lower everyone's stress quotient. Relevant here is this observation by an academic veteran of factory work:

> Workers' interests are wholly identified in union leaders' minds with the capitalist system. Union officials therefore believe, along with many rank-and-file members, that workers' interests are best served by the prosperity of the employing company, which in turn, leaders believe, requires the company's near-exclusive control of the conduct of its business.[11]

This, of course, requires much sensitive labor collaboration with progressive management forces, a uniquely American style of comanagement that high-level labor leaders worry may be fast leaving the current union-management scene (see Chapter 4).

MANAGING HEARTACHE

Many local union officers I have known shoulder a remarkable responsibility as lay counselors for the personal problems of their members. As such, they are asked to hear out and offer advice on marital problems, parent-child conflicts, in-law problems, alcoholism, and scores of other personal difficulties. The president of a Teamster Union local explains:

> You'd be surprised at the calls we get about family problems. . . . I got one recently from a guy who was in tears because his kid was "a little retarded" and he didn't know what to do. They come over

> *to us in the shops with these problems or they call us. Sometimes they talk for fifteen minutes about nothing before they break down and tell us what's wrong. Sometimes we can only offer advice or sympathy, but a lot of the time we have programs we can refer them to.*[12]

Positioned by their role between the foreman and the dues payer, many shop stewards and local union officers find—sometimes to their surprise—that considerable stress relief help is expected from them, regardless of their lack of credentials for offering intimate counsel to perplexed coworkers. There is little notice taken of the related increase in personal psychological stress experienced by the typecast helpers themselves: A former labor education student of mine, a thirty-eight-year-old local business agent, offered this analysis:

> *They dump on us, all the time. They don't think anything of unloading on us anything and everything . . . the things they tell us! I tell you, it can really get to you . . . you have to keep a wall up so as not to get hurt. You have to let them know that they can only go so far in reaching you, in finding you, before they bump into your wall. It's the only way you can stay sane yourself, what with them unloading their problems on you all the time.*[13]

Similarly, another former student, a thirty-four-year-old local union president, explained his misgivings about his lay counselor role:

> *I'm not comfortable making referrals. Instead I kind of offer 10¢ worth of crackerbarrel philosophy, and hope that that helps some. I just don't know enough to make referrals. . . . I don't trust enough in what I know to go out on a limb and send anyone to this or that outfit. . . .*[14]

With all of this, however, the role cannot be denied—and local union officials do the best they can: Rank-and-filers *demand* this particular sort of stress relief from their leaders, and "make do" themselves with the best of it.

MANAGING ELECTION TURNOVER

Another major source of workplace stress involves politics, an exceedingly well-studied art in the local unions. To borrow a typology from steelworker Charles Spencer, men seek local union office for at least seven major reasons:

- It is a way to call attention to one's self, and thereby to angle for a promotion into a supervisory position.

- It can provide a small salary supplement in the form of expenses or a nominal monthly check.

- It can relieve the routine of daily work and actually provide days off to attend a meeting or conference or to perform "union business."

- It can expand a worker's off-work life experience, as through attendance at union conventions in distant cities, membership in city-wide charity committees, participation in college and high school forums, and the out-of-the-ordinary like.

- It can satisfy a personal desire to be of service, to make a difference, to invest one's life with meaning: "Being part of an established and respected movement that has a reputation for contributing to the welfare of the workers is a source of considerable social satisfaction and fulfillment for many officers of local unions."[15]

- It can lead to a promotion into the salaried ranks in higher bodies of the labor movement. (Suspicious dues payers, however, often allege that "applicants from universities, or, more often, the sons, brothers, in-laws, or nephews of union leaders are moved into these positions, without regard to the 'eligible' local union functionaries.")[16]

Holding a local union office, in short, provides a distinct standing in the workplace, and its different points of origin help insure periodic ballot-time stress and controversy.

Stress and ballot-box turnover of incumbents are aided by rifts among the membership, as illustrated by this account from a union old-timer who notices a generation gap:

> The young kids . . . I don't see how a steward can defend them. I mean what can a steward say for somone who just wants to take Fridays off? . . . what can a steward do for a kid who wakes up and just doesn't feel like coming to work; doesn't bother to call; doesn't even bother to make up a story? . . . they don't make a demand. They don't want to fight. All they want to do is say "Fuck it." . . . They're sure they're not going to stay here. They think of us as a bunch of old farts who wasted our lives in a factory.[17]

Another source of ballot-box turbulence connects to chronic dissatisfaction with nationally bargained contract terms:

> *Workplace reaction generally runs a narrow range from the cyni-*
> *cal "we were sold down the river," to the resentful "it was rammed*
> *down our throats," to the shrug that translates into "what can we*
> *do? It's better than a strike." Even the local union officers avoid*
> *defending the contract if they plan to run for reelection. Only the*
> *international union's staff give it unstinted praise.*[18]

Election politics, of course, harbor their own contradictions, as some
local union officers will rush to be the first to hail a new contract as
"the greatest!" in order to curry favor with attentive and appreciative
elements at international union headquarters.

Above all, local union politics pivot around judgments of service
rendered in the daily go-round at work. Workers tell me they add up
the score and assess how well incumbents helped them when they
found themselves scrapping with foremen or pinning their hopes on
the grievance procedure.

Dues payers especially profit here from the shop steward's considerable ballot-box vulnerability, and use this as leverage in insuring
satisfactory grievance handling:

> *Workers, and frequently with good reason, will suspect that there*
> *is a mercenary or ulterior motive behind any significant act of a*
> *union or management official. "What's the angle?" . . . But, in the*
> *case of stewards, finding proof isn't that hard because the*
> *steward operates in an open environment where his constituents*
> *can observe him constantly, something they cannot do with higher*
> *officials. . . . In the absence of an entrenched bureaucracy at the local*
> *union level it is not all that hard to defeat a steward when his*
> *constituents become dissatisfied with his performance.*[29]

On their own part, incumbents have their own legalistic sort of leverage. For example:

> *. . . considerably fewer than 10 percent of the union membership*
> *attended more than one of the regular union business meetings a*
> *year. . . . Because one of the requirements for eligibility to union*
> *office was that a nominee have attended at least five meetings*
> *during the year preceding nominations in November, poor at-*
> *tendance also meant probably fewer than 5 percent of the total*

> *membership in the local were even eligible. . . . And approximately half of that 5 percent were incumbents and their hangers-on.*[26]

As well, challengers run a risk of more personalized attention:

> *Jobs out of many [building trade] locals are to a large extent a matter of patronage and good reputation. Supers' in-laws get work, and good men get work, most of the time. The business agents who run the halls can punish men whom they feel need punishing by not sending them out, or get even with men who might have opposed them in the previous local elections by not sending them out.*[21]

To be sure, retribution of this sort is less common in large than in small locals, and all locals are under the supervision of the International: "But who goes out on what jobs is much too small a matter for International scrutiny."[22]

MANAGING DISSENT

Up to this point we have been assuming that "everything is on the up and up," and that a democratically run local union accommodates, even if it may not welcome, hard-fought stressful election contests for union posts. When the opposite is true, when challenges to entrenched local leadership are viewed as unhealthy for insurgents, the accompanying stressors can go out of sight.

Typical of election strife is this account of an unsuccessful 1978 effort to unseat a rather notorious Teamsters Union local president:

> *As they visited plants, the insurgents were followed, forced to match their eloquence against the quiet persuasion of "two or three guys in a car, who just sit there and watch." . . . [their candidate for the local's presidency] was beaten up three years ago at a union meeting, the fate of others who have spoken out during or after elections . . . [insurgents] campaigned only in groups, heeding the warnings that they'd be "taken care of."*[23]

In turn, labor leaders at the level of the national union generally represent the local union election scene as one of a fairly reasonable, and certainly representative, character:

> Bernard Henderson, spokesman for the Teamsters Union: "We have 730 locals. There are people who run good locals and people

who run bad locals. That's a fact of life. But all our local officials are elected. If members don't like their officials they can elect new ones.[24]

Perhaps, and then again, perhaps not. . . . The related turmoil here resonates as a stressor of considerable consequence on and off the job, as the worried wives and children of various dissidents can attest.

When local union rebels do occasionally make headway, it is generally by focusing on substantial arguments the rank and file has with distant and seemingly officious higher-ups. Typical is an ongoing and very heated argument between Teamsters Union headquarters and one of its locals allied with the 3,000-member national dissident group, Teamsters for a Democratic Union (TDU): An employer introduced new production standards in 1976 and unilaterally began suspending workers whom it said were low producers. The local filed a grievance, citing a provision in the master freight agreement that allows companies to set "reasonable work standards subject to agreement and approval with the local union." Shortly thereafter, a joint committee of union and industry representatives sought to "cut a deal" seemingly satisfactory to both sides: They awarded back pay to the suspended men, but also authorized the company to continue. TDU, insisting that the joint committee had no right to make that decision without the local's approval, has taken the entire case to court.

Across the country, local union dissidents capitalize on these sorts of bread-and-butter issues, as in the following typical accounts:

- When plant closings were announced in late 1977, steel union "insurgents" called for "immediate federal investigation of the industry as a first step toward public control over job reductions. This call was not taken up by the union's International Office."[25]

- ". . . in many instances, the dissidents have been much more aggressive than the union officials in fighting to help truckers hang on to their jobs. For example, when [a company takeover of another trucking firm was proposed], teamster member Paul Sheperd and a number of his fellow drivers in Pittsburgh were threatened with relocation to Sharon, Pa. They decided to fight the move.

  "'TDU put us in touch with lawyers. They helped our stewards collect the information to build our case. The union filed some papers, but they didn't seem very interested,' recalls Mr. Sheperd.

... The drivers lost after a 14-month struggle, but TDU picked up some members, including Mr. Sheperd, who now drives out of Sharon, Pa., for the new owner."[26]

Convinced by long experience that a hard-boiled membership is best reached by a better pocketbook idea rather than through ideological appeals, local union dissidents promote stress-inducing labor militancy that focuses on wages, hours, and working conditions: Every possible workplace grievance is championed with unusual vigor and vehemence to better help dissidents win (rare) ballot-box upsets over entrenched and more pacific incumbents.

A keener sense of the turmoil here can be gained from the seemingly contradictory position of a thirteen-year veteran driver and former shop steward, Steven Smith of Pittsburgh, who talks like a dissident and complains that his international union administration keeps dues payers in the dark:

> But ask Mr. Smith about . . . TDU and he snorts, "I don't belong to any outside activities." When a TDU leader spoke at a local union meeting a couple of years ago, Mr. Smith waved an American flag and sang "God Bless America" to drown him out.[27]

Not surprisingly, then, TDU and a similar dissident group, PROD (Professional Over the Road Drivers), can only claim fewer than 10,000 members in the 2,3000,000-member union and hope to elect only 40 or 50 delegates to the International's 1981 convention with its 2,000 delegates.[28]

Still, the likelihood remains strong that local union politics will long reverberate here with deeply felt argumentation: Typical are these sentiments of a thirty-year veteran driver:

> Al Barkett, Teamster member: A lot of other guys have the desire [to join TDU]. But they don't do it because they figured it would be an exercise in futility. You know, you don't fight City Hall. . . . A lot of people feel what's the use. . . . There's fear involved, too. I mean, you don't want to be found off a New Jersey pier, do you? . . . I'll bet you not more than 30 percent of the members really support Fitzsimmons and the other bosses in the union. The other 70 percent all have mixed emotions like I do.[29]

Later, explaining his reaction as a nondissident to high-level union criticism of the dissidents, Barkett sounds a note I have often heard in other similar union settings:

. . . sometimes I'm not proud of the people who speak for us. No, I'm not proud of them. I get so goddamn steamed up sometimes. Like when Fitzsimmons at the Las Vegas Convention [in 1976] told the dissidents [PROD] that they could go to hell. That's bullshit. What's the definition of a dissident? Dissidents founded our country. Who the hell is he to tell them to go to hell? [30]

This sort of feisty defense of the underdog, this insistence on the legitimacy of dissent helps keep local union affairs far more volatile than many incumbent officers might prefer.

REFORMS

Close to 20 million dues payers, organized in nearly 190 international unions and over 70,000 locals, know their own local union scene with keen intimacy and judicious concern. Outsiders, however, can still help with reform suggestions to help enlarge the reform dialogue going on within the labor movement itself and to confirm the persistence of constructive interest without.

The business community, for example, could promote a more balanced image of itself *and* make a substantial contribution to stress reduction at work through its consideration of these two union-related items:

• Business could join with unions in *facilitating and subsidizing the upgrading of local union skills at antistress tasks;* for example, an agreement between Ohio Bell and the Communications Workers Union provides for the company to pay for the first day of two-day stewards' training classes in the policing of the union contract. The union president reports that "both the company and the union are in agreement that trained stewards make for better labor-management relations, quicker settlement of grievances at the first step, and reduced friction on the job." [31]

• Business could also encourage the highest levels of the corporate hierarchy, including members of the board of directors as well as key management officials, to accompany union officers on *annual union-guided tours of the workplace* (the president of the Communications Workers Union, after first lambasting "theoreticians cloistered in an ivory tower [who are] totally ignorant of the genuine experience of industrial employment," goes on to contend that "it would help a great deal . . . if the top decision-makers in management—not just the first line supervisors—would take the trouble to find out what is really going on at the job level.") [32]

Similarly, labor's officials, negligent themselves in some aspects of this complex subject, might give open-minded consideration to three related reforms:

• Expansion of the type of *labor-management collaboration* pioneered in the UAW-GM Quality of Worklife Program: "Among its tasks is the development of joint, cooperative experiments and projects designed to improve the quality of worklife, with an eye toward worker participation in the decision-making process on the job . . . improving the quality of worklife projects helps create a climate in which cool reason and judgment override anger and emotion in working out controversial problems. It therefore has a beneficial impact upon the total collective bargaining relationship. . . . Successful projects (and not all succeed) could begin to alter intrinsically the decades old shopworn system of management-worker relations and the philosophy underlying the concept of 'scientific management.' It could enhance the dignity of the worker on his job, involve him significantly in the decision-making process, improve the opportunity for heightened satisfaction and move toward a democratization of the workplace not heretofore achieved."[33]

• Improvement of relations with new (first-job) younger workers through a larger role in *high school and community college vocational programs*; for example, the locals could extend across the country a pilot project similar to the one that in 1977 involved five community colleges. With a demonstration grant from the Department of Labor, the two-year schools created *Education-Works Councils* that brought together school officials, employers, union representatives, and members of the public to guide the colleges in new course offerings, the assessment of ongoing courses, and so forth.[34]

• *Redesign of the "lay counselor" preparation of local union officers and all international union functionaries with a direct service role;* for example, union students of mine, when asked if they would appreciate the opportunity to take a union-financed adult education short course in mental health "listening skills" or in the range of treatment modalities available for local mental health gains strongly endorsed the idea. Several asked how they could learn more about Gamblers Anonymous, Al-Anon, the Marriage Encounter Movement, and so on.

Whatever the details, reforms *must* be grounded in recognition of the antistress orientation of most local union leaders—laymen committed to making things more democratic and smoother in their place of work: " . . . the whole purpose of a strong union," a local union president explains, "is so you can clear things up with a phone call. . . ." [35]

SUMMARY

A judicious consideration of the stress-relieving and stress-aggravating aspects of the local union must begin with—and never lose sight of—the contention of a number of blue-collarites I have known (and nearly all old-timers I have read about) that "any union is better than no union at all." Decades of near destitution are still well within the memories of many gray-haired blue-collarites, and they assiduously keep their fond memories of struggle alive:

> "The problem," says union Vice President Pat Duffy, who works in the toolroom, "is that we won all the fights twenty years ago. Ah but we were the young turks then." . . . McManus [the local president] says something similar. "We win everything too automatically these days. But it's not really winning. Things you get at the table are forgotten two days later. Sometimes I wish they'd fire ten people. Then we'd really have to fight. That would recharge the batteries for the next twenty years." [36]

Many rank-and-filers, as is well known, take their local unions for granted, while some are not reluctant to tell the world that "it isn't worth a shit!" Some condemn the locals for caving in to management; others, for excessive militancy. Some use the local as a convenient scapegoat for all of their workplace disappointments; others try to use it to advance covert career goals of their own.

Membership passivity and incumbent political machinations are commonplace, though the ballot's availability and the close scrutiny of coworkers help keep many locals dynamic and responsive. Rank-and-filers generally applaud their locals for having raised their living standards, and for having increased their job security. Above all, however, local unions are valued for their rule-making and rule-policing roles in workplace governance, and for their stress-reducing maintenance of industrial peace—with all that this implies for general well-being at work.

NOTES

1. Charles Spencer, *Blue Collar: An Internal Examination of the Workplace* (Chicago: Lakeside Charter Books, 1977), pp. 1-2. "The approach here is that any and all definitions, symbols, portrayals, statements, examples, tables and theories of blue collar workers, must be tested out on the proving grounds of the workplace. If it won't hold up there, it's probably phony" (p. 3.).

2. Richard M. Pfeffer, *Working for Capitalism* (New York: Columbia University Press, 1979), p. 120.

3. Al Nash, "The Local Union: Center of Life in the UAW," *Dissent*, Fall 1978, p. 399.

4. David Fitzmaurice, president of the International Union of Electrical Workers, as quoted in Nick Kotz, "Can Labor's Tired Leaders Deal with a Troubled Movement?" *New York Times Magazine*, September 4, 1977, p. 11.

5. Spencer, *Blue Collar*, p. 92. "If the adult population of the nation were subject to a comparable system of disciplines, it would translate, roughly, into 45 million citations per year!" (p. 93).

6. Nash, "The Local Union," p. 404. See also Duane Beeler and Harry Kurshcenbaum, *Roles of the Labor Leader* (Chicago: Union Representative, 1969).

7. Peter J. Sampson, "Cancer Deaths Rise at GM Plant," *The News World*, August 31, 1978, p. 9-A. Labor is pressing for an OSHA ruling that will assure access to employee medical records and other relevant exposure and medical data, provided that the worker gives his written consent: See "OSHA Tries to Expose On-Job Medical Files," *Business Week*, August 7, 1978, pp. 28-29.

8. Sampson, "Cancer Deaths" p. 9-A.

9. Seymour Melman, "Beating 'Swords' into Subways," *New York Times Magazine*, November 19, 1978, p. 102.

10. As quoted in Richard E. Walton, "What's the Bottom Line?" *The Wharton Magazine*, Spring 1979, p. 41.

11. Pfeffer, *Working for Capitalism*, p. 125.

12. As quoted in Steven Brill, *The Teamsters* (New York: Simon and Shuster, 1978), p. 178.

13. As quoted in Arthur B. Shostak, "Psychiatry Issues and Organized Labor," *Journal of Occupational Medicine* 21, No. 1 (January 1979): 50.

14. *Ibid.* See also Arthur B. Shostak, "Blue-Collar Mental Health: Changes Since 1968," *Journal of Occupational Medicine*, November 1974, pp. 741-743.

15. Spencer, *Blue Collar*, p. 105.

16. *Ibid.*

17. As quoted in Barbara Garson, *All the Livelong Day: The Meaning and Demeaning of Routine Work* (New York: Penguin, 1975), p. 68.

18. Spencer, *Blue Collar* pp. 121-122.

19. Nash, "The Local Union," pp. 401-402.

20. Pfeffer, *Working for Capitalism*, p. 117.

21. Mike Cherry, *On High Steel: The Education of an Ironworker* (New York: Ballantine, 1974), p. 29.

22. *Ibid.*

23. See in this connection Alan Barnes, "Reform Marks Teamster Elections," *In These Times*, December 20-26, 1978, p. 7. See also Dan La Botz, "Teamster Davids Plan to Bury Goliath," *In These Times*, November 1-7, 1978, p. 7; Michael Gillespie, "McBride Steels Union Against Dissent," *In These Times*, October 4-10, 1978; Matt Witt, "Two Reform Groups Take on the Teamsters," *Working Papers*, July/August 1978, pp. 10-14.

24. As quoted in Urban C. Lehner, "Trucking Turmoil," *Wall Street Journal*, March 9, 1979, p. 12.

25. William Kornblum, "Crisis in the Steel Industry," *Dissent*, Spring 1978, p. 149.

26. Lehner, "Trucking Turmoil," p. 12. See also H.W. Benson, *Democratic Rights for Union Members* (New York: Association for Union Democracy, 1979).

27. *Ibid.*

28. "Dissidents in the Teamsters are Gaining Clout," *Business Week*, November 13, 1978, pp. 136, 139.

29. As quoted in Brill, *The Teamsters*, p. 278.

30. *Ibid.*, p. 239. On the fears that "keep the lid on politics in the factory," see Pfeffer, *Working for Capitalism*, p. 184.

31. Glenn E. Watts, "The Work Ethic Is Alive in America," *Viewpoint* 8, No. 3 (1978): 10.

32. *Ibid.*

33. Irving Bluestone, vice-president, UAW, "Improving the Quality of Workplace," unpublished paper prepared for the First National Seminar on Industrial Rights in the Corporation, New York, May 9, 1978, pp. 13, 16. See also Daniel Zwerdling, "Workplace Democracy: A Strategy for Survival," *The Progressive*, August 1978, p. 18; Irving Bluestone, "Work Humanization in Practice: What Can Labor Do?" in W.J. Heisler and J.W. Houck, eds., *A Matter of Dignity: Inquiries into the Humanization of Work* (Notre Dame, IN: University of Notre Dame Press, 1977).

34. William A. Harper, "The Workers' College," *Change*, May 1977, p. 52.

35. Dick McManus, president, Local 8-149, Oil Chemical and Atomic Workers International Union, as quoted in Barbara Garson, *All the Livelong Day* (see note 17).

36. As quoted in Garson, *All the Livelong Day*, pp. 68-69.

READING:
HOW REALLY "DIFFERENT"
ARE THE YOUNGER MEN?
AND, SO WHAT?

When I recently asked trade union students of mine at the George Meany Center for Labor Studies (AFL-CIO) to analyze and prescribe for the situation of their younger members, I received the following instructive response from Andrew A. Cuvo, an officer of a local of the International Brotherhood of Electrical Workers Union (IBEW):

As new members come into the unions, we hope to have enough work for all of them. The recent decline in the building trades industry has created different types of problems for all those working in the trades. One of the problems we have in I.B.E.W. Local 367 is getting the younger members of the local to accept the work that is available to them. The problem is that the work requires some traveling and the younger members refuse to travel to obtain work.

After serving their four-year apprenticeship and working locally during a four- to five-year building boom, the younger members had gotten used to working close to home. Now that there is very little work in the area, these men don't want to go where the work is. They collect unemployment benefits as long as they can pick up a few side jobs, and struggle to make ends meet. Sooner or later they run out of money and find themselves in a position to lose their cars, homes, and families, and they still refuse to travel.

The older members of the local (thirty-five and older) are willing to work out of town because that was their way of life before the short-lived boom in this area. As a result, they are earning $25,000 to $35,000 per year while those who won't travel are making $160 per week for a thirty-week unemployment period.

Lifestyle changes for the younger members of the local are going to be unavoidable if they are to keep their heads above water financially. A reorientation program will have to be made available to these men. The type of program necessary would have to deal not only with helping the men accept travel as part of their work, but also with helping them deal with the stress that traveling puts on their marriage and family life.

In the first part of the "job reorientation" the men would have to be told of the practicalities of travel and working away from home. The leaders of the reorientation group would have to point out advantages that are not of a monetary nature: the men already know what they will be earning. The lifestyle that goes with working out of town has to be presented honestly; not only are there advantages such as money, comradeship, mobility, and a degree of freedom from the everyday life at home, there are also disadvantages, mainly driving and being away from the family for four nights. The men also have to be told what the prospects for finding work close to home are. Perhaps the men would be more willing to travel if they were convinced that the work situation isn't expected to get any better here in the near future. They could be hanging on to hopes of being able to work nearby if they can just wait a little longer. Realizing that their hopes aren't going to materialize might force them to accept the lifestyle of traveling for work.

If we can get the men back to work, we have to keep our channels of communication open until they have become adjusted to their new routines. This brings us to the second part of the program—helpihg the men deal with the stresses that traveling puts on their marriages and family life. A discussion group, led by someone who could direct or guide the exchange of ideas, might be helpful. The men could air their problems or anxieties and learn how other men in the same position deal with them. This group would help by bringing out into the open the problems that exist and by showing the men that they are not unique in their situations. Knowing that other men found ways to handle the stresses of working away from home might help the men to cope with the situation a little better than they would without the group experience.

Having the union's membership gainfully employed is a primary goal of the leadership. By introducing a reorientation program to get the younger members of this local back to work, we hope to accomplish this. The local would then be functioning as it should and we could direct more of our energies toward reform outside of our local's internal affairs. We have to deal with our own problem areas before we can even hope to be instrumental in resolving society's ails. Our long-range goal of equal employment for women and minority group members could then be worked for more actively by this local's membership.

Andrew A. Cuvo was born in Easton, Pennsylvania, in 1934. The son of a millwright, he has been active in county-level union activities for many years in a wide range of posts, and has served since 1972 as the chief executive officer of Local 367 of the International Brotherhood of Electrical Workers, an organization of approximately 600 construction members.

Mr. Cuvo has attended East Stroudsberg State College, Penn State, Northampton Area Community College, and the George Meany Center for Labor Studies, from which he expects to earn a B.A. degree in 1979.

4

BLUE-COLLAR INTERNATIONAL UNIONS: NATIONAL ISSUES

If one talks to any worker long enough, and candidly enough, one discovers that his loyalty to the union is not simply economic. One may even be able to show him that, on a strictly cost-benefit analysis, measuring income lost from strikes and jobs lost as a result of contract terms, the cumulative economic benefits are delusions. It won't matter. In the end, he will tell you, the union is the only institution that ensures and protects his "dignity" as a worker, that prevents him from losing his personal identity and from being transformed into an infinitesimal unit in one huge and abstract "factor of production."

IRVING KRISTOL*

America's unionized blue-collarites are involved with labor at three distinct levels, each with its own record where stress is concerned: Of greatest significance to rank-and-filers are *local union* realities, followed by *international union* affairs, and thereafter, by the doings of the AFL-CIO (110 affiliates and 13,500,000 members).

As I have tried to make clear in previous chapters, organized labor profoundly influences *every* aspect of workplace existence (compensation levels, job security, job safety, worker self-esteem, and so forth), as well as many after-work matters (including the provision of health

---

*"Understanding Trade Unionism," *Wall Street Journal*, October 23, 1978, p. 24.

care at union clinics and the publication of labor newspapers that go
into millions of blue-collar households). Accordingly, I focus here on
significant links between blue-collar stress and issues that go beyond
any particular workplace or local union. I discuss antilabor campaigns, union corruption, labor politics, and labor-management relations, closing with a few reform possibilities worth attention from
those who, in the words of series editor Alan A. McLean, are eager to
"reduce unhealthy environmental social stimuli for the employee at
risk."

ANTILABOR CAMPAIGNS

A tally sheet of the last few years would include the following struggles, all of them likely to persist for years to come:

• AFL-CIO lobbyists lost their bid in 1978 for a reform of the National Labor Relations Board's procedures that make it difficult to
defend workers discharged for union activity: " . . . big business won
what they correctly call the great labor war of 1978."[1]

• The Council on Union Free Environment, a new union-fighting
affiliate of the National Association of Manufacturers, has begun to
release critical studies of labor, such as a 1979 report which contends
that government figures may overstate total union membership by as
much as 10 percent, or over 2,000,000. (While agreeing that precise
figures are difficult to obtain, the government insists the results are as
likely to be understated as overstated.)[2]

• The National Right to Work Legal Defense Foundation (NRWLDF)
has taken out a $100,000 serious of antiunion ads in intellectual opinion-
shaping magazines, such as *The New Republic*, *The New York Review
of Books*, *Commentary*, and others. ("We'd like to reach more of a
working audience," says publicity director James Taylor, "perhaps in
magazines like *True*. We want working people to know that we exist
and that we'd like to help them.") Drawing on a $3,200,000 annual
budget and a staff of fifty-five, the NRWLDF has commissioned emotionally charged ads that relate case histories of sympathetic, independent working peple who just want to be left alone: A critic concedes
that the ads "effectively tap and encourage the American public's
growing disenchantment with organized labor and its loss of strength
among workers themselves."[3]

• Since the mid-1970s, four new antiunion groups have emerged; the Center on National Labor Policy, for example, provides legal help for "victims of union abuse." Americans Against Union Control of Government, with a budget of $3 million and a staff of twenty, opposes prounion measures in state legislatures. The Committee to Defeat the Union Bosses' Candidates and the Fund to Stop Big Labor both fight unionism among public employees and diversify when appropriate to oppose union security in any form.[4]

Given these developments—and many more of the same sort—it is not hard to grasp what Machinist Union president William W. Winpisinger means when he grimly contends that "the trade union movement in this country gets out of bed every morning, putting on its cast iron underwear and a shield around its jugular, because the enemy is after it every minute of every waking hour."[5]

The so-called right-to-work effort, or more accurately, the antiunion-shop campaign, especially adds to the national quotient of labor survival stress. Coordinated by the National Right-To-Work Committee, "the most powerful of all these groups—and the centerpiece of the current war against unions," this campaign has helped increase the number of states (from seventeen in 1955 [when it was formed] to twenty states today) that have a ban on all arrangements but the open shop; under the ban, employees may receive union-won wages and benefits even if they are not union members. The committee, with a staff of sixty-eight and a budget of more than $6 million, specializes in direct mail and ads (8,000,000 pieces sent to defeat the 1977 Labor Reform Act, and forty full-page newspaper ads taken in the home states of senators who favored the bill). As well, it has two full-time and five occasional lobbyists on Capital Hill.[6]

Typical of recent campaigns, though handled locally rather than by the National Committee, was the exceedingly bitter fight which had Missourians listening for months in 1978 to this radio commercial urging approval of a proposed antiunion shop law:

> *Unions have done a lot for us. They have disrupted business, paralyzed public services, and pushed up costs and prices. Unions have kept qualified workers out of work, forced them out of our state. When labor unions grow too strong, they grow corrupt and greedy. It happens every time. Vote "yes" on Amendment 23. Keep unions under control in Missouri.*[7]

As the November vote date grew closer in the nation's eighth most industrial state, the prolaw radio and television commercials talked less about their opposition to a requirement of membership in a union shop and more about labor bosses, violence, and "crippling strikes that . . . take money out of your pocket."[8] (Early in the year, polls had shown a two-to-one vote for the proposed right-to-work law with very heavy antilabor support even in union families. On election day, however, the law went down to defeat by a nearly three-to-two margin in a record turnout of voters in a nonpresidential election. Labor's successful rallying of rank-and-filers was given special credit by observers for this dramatic win.)

To better protect themselves against stinging criticisms of their unions, blue-collarites have developed a host of stress-reducing strategies; significant is the practice of accenting the positive: Blue-collarites dwell on what it is *they* want from organized labor and get, *regardless* of the preferences and judgments of nonunion outsiders. This is not to say that labor's faults are overlooked. It is quite the contrary; both the rank and file and the officials pride themselves on their "insider" grasp of labor's various and nefarious shortcomings. They just do not see that it is anybody else's business, and they profoundly suspect the motives of critics . . . whether on the right, middle, or left.

Above all, the men value *results*, regardless of what the rest of the country chooses to make of the deal. For example, consider this case of justice sought and won:

> Since container shipping was introduced in 1956, vessels that once required 100 men a week to unload are handled overnight by 30 or 40 longshoremen. From a membership of 50,000 in 1952 the union in New York City has fallen to 11,800 in 1978: In a series of bitter, protracted strikes, the union won from the shipping industry key job-security concessions that guaranteed pay of $8.00 an hour for 2,090 hours of work a year per man, whether there was that much work or not, whether a man worked or did not.[9]

Even when the "big scene" abounds, then, with media and public censure as often as at present, the stress otherwise engendered appears to be reduced for workers who can imagine how it might have been if labor had not won key organizing wars a mere four decades ago and thereby helped bring "due process" into industrial relations.

When "what if" flights of frightening fancy are not enough, blue-collarites can call on various other stress-reducing ploys:

- Some will insist that the papers lie, that the media are all pro-management and never tell the union's side of the story.
- Some will insist that labor is doing as well as can be expected given its enemies and the nature of power distribution in a capitalistic society.
- Some will insist that labor is doing no worse than any other sector of society, all of which, . . . the church, the universities, the hospitals, . . . have their own share of crooks, charlatans, frauds, "bosses" and even "goons."
- Some will insist that things are a helluva lot better today than during the Depression decade, and that makes everything appear in a better light.

Many of course, will move easily from one to another of these defensive lines of argument, persuaded at their core that the little man is utterly indefensible without a mass organization. A frustrating puzzle to labor's many enemies, this gut-level dedication of an influential core of rank-and-filers (by no means all!) explains much of labor's ability to survive even when, as today, the big scene appears largely a bleak scene.

UNION CORRUPTION

For all of their worldly wise cynicism and bold front, many blue-collarites are distressed by their inside, off-the-record knowledge of union-linked kickbacks, extortion, deals, threats, beatings, and murders. The story is an old one, and its bizarre components can make even the worst of television crime and violence seem more like a flaccid family hour in comparison.

As an index of the subject's complexity and contradictions, however, dissidents seldom try to unseat incumbents only on charges of alleged Mafia ties or criminal hookups: Such accusations often backfire on their users by stirring rank-and-file admiration for the reputed macho power and deadly amorality of larger-than-life labor outlaws.

Jimmy Hoffa's image, since his mysterious disappearance in 1975, is instructive as rank-and-file Teamsters continue to hold him in high regard despite his prison term and his notorious links with underworld syndicate captains:

> . . . most Teamster members are disarmed by their ideological conviction that theft and crookedness are in the order of things. . . .

> *Al Barkett, a typical over-the-road union member, says of Hoffa,*
> *"Sure he stole, but everybody does. He did us good; that's what*
> *counts." Another member is reported to have said, "I don't care*
> *what Jimmy Hoffa does with my $4 a month* [it's at least $18 for
> over-the-road now]—*he can shoot craps on the White House lawn*
> *if he wants to—so long as he keeps up the present conditions."*[10]

Burly, bull strong, earthy, and contemptuous of authority, Hoffa met
the bill in a way that reformers still find hard to match:

> *He had the toughness they admire, and they remember him as the*
> *hard-nosed bargainer who had lifted them out of penury and*
> *brought them contracts that enabled many to earn $500 a week or*
> *more.*[11]

This bravado mix of buccaneering and worker gains helps explain
why Hoffa's heirs shrug at the underworld's continued presence in
parts of the 2.3 million member Teamsters empire—even while respec-
ting the threat that would-be reformers may exit from the Teamsters'
world "horizontally," as Hoffa apparently did.

Those inclined to relieve stressors here by grasping at rationalizations have always had many to choose from:

> *If* [a union official] *was cruel, it was against those even more cruel.*
> *If "family" members stole, it was from those who were greedy. If*
> *they became rich, they acted without hypocrisy in a world where*
> *bankers exploited the poor. If they killed, they risked their own*
> *lives according to their own code of criminal honor. . . . If* [they]
> *collaborated with gangsters, so went the fable, you had to fight*
> *fire with fire to build a union.*[12]

Similarly, a concerned journalist's recent research into fifty-three Teamsters locals operating in the New York area had him condemn ten for
brazen corruption, twenty-five or so for mild corruption, and exoner-
ate the dozen that remained:

> *It was not a terrific box score—and certainly not equal to what*
> *would likely be found at the United Auto Workers locals.*[13]

More interesting yet, however, was the journalist's insistence that
"perhaps [this box score] is no worse than the record of American
businessmen in handling their expense accounts, in filling out their tax
returns, or in other activities with comparably open opportunities for
corruption."[14]

Despite the availability of these stress-reducing rationalizations, a number of blue-collarites make an effort to "kick the bums the hell out." Far more often than outsiders know, blue-collarites respond by rebelling against, and warring on allegedly crooked incumbents. With all the courage, tenacity, and outrage that reformers can possess, they remain heavily disadvantaged. Prior to labor law reforms in 1959, they were crippled by union constitution clauses that outlawed caucuses, suppressed free speech, curbed handbills, and penalized dissidents who took their unions into court. While most of these practices are now illegal, many persist by subterfuge. As well, recent circuit court rulings hurt: Damage claims have been upheld against unions and their members for wildcatting and stranger-picketing; this is a legal holding that increases the requirement on internationals to control unruly members and locals.

Not surprisingly, then, H.W. Benson, a writer and reform activist, concludes that "ordinary trade-union activity is simply not enough."[15] Instead, this lifelong union reformer calls for *vigorous* public support for union dissidents, *strict* enforcement of existing laws for union democracy, and *emphatic* use of existing laws against crime in the labor movement.

LABOR UNIONISTS AND POLITICS

Blue-collarites receive a steady and skillful series of political messages from their unions and the AFL-CIO. For example:

> *A bill which could threaten the basic democratic rights of all Americans, and which contains several provisions especially dangerous to trade unionists, has been passed by the U.S. Senate and is now being considered by the House of Representatives.*

> *. . . There are many dangerous provisions in S. 1437, but of particular concern to trade unionists are the two sections of the bill which deal with extortion and blackmail. These crimes are so broadly defined that they will permit wholesale federal intervention against strikers, and make strikers liable to penalties of up to 10 years in prison and/or a $100,000 fine.*

> *. . . The seeds of repression have been written into the Senate Bill in the guise of reform. . . . Trade unionists should write to their own representatives, and ask them to oppose the bill.*[16]

Other targets of the labor political effort commonly include the right wing and its corporate political allies, along with the right-to-work proponents, the enemies of a strong OSHA, opponents of national health insurance, and so on. At the same time, arguments in the labor press and at labor gatherings propose the formation of a job-creating national energy program, creation of a consumer affairs agency, passage of a new labor law reform act, passage of stronger tariff protections against imported goods that appear to cost the jobs of American workers, and so forth.

Blue-collar responses here remain *very* uneven with workers proving to be increasingly independent minded. Unionists *will* rally when a political contest strikes them as clear-cut and critical, as evident since 1958 by labor's win over the right-to-work forces in six of seven state referendums. After analyzing labor's latest success (Missouri, November 1978) a political analyst has offered two relevant propositions:

1. *While the public and even union members themselves may not give enthusiastic approval to every aspect of the labor movement, they are firm in their resistance to those who would dismantle the basic arrangements of our industrial democracy.*

2. *Labor's political machinery, if limited in some of its capacities, can mount a potent effort when the unions are united around what they take to be issues of survival.*[17]

At most other times, however, blue-collarites appear to take labor's advice and recommendations as only *one* among many inputs to weigh: This refusal to be taken for granted is both a measure of multiple tugs on their vote (concerning age, locality, ethnic, or religious priorities) and an indicator of their calculating wariness of Big Labor's (veiled?) agenda.

To be sure, there remain many congressional districts, some of them pivotal in federal or state election outcomes, in which the endorsement of the Committee on Political Education (COPE), the AFL-CIO's political arm, or the backing of one or more major international unions makes *the* difference. Nevertheless, the more common situation nowadays is one which has both the rank-and-filers I know and students of the subject agree that labor's vote-shaping power wanes. Skepticism waxes strong, instead, about labor's influence over an increasingly independent-minded union membership. While dues payers may be learning more about politics from labor than ever before true, they seem no more persuaded to vote labor's way—or, for that matter, to vote at all—in the aftermath of labor's best effort in the matter.

LABOR-MANAGEMENT RELATIONS

Two contradictory forces are at work in the area of labor-management relations, with the outcome in the 1980s anything but clear: On one hand, stress-wracked hostilities so fierce as to resemble class warfare at times shake the entire scene. On the other hand, increasingly powerful incentives in the need to meet global economic competition and to earn productivity increases *could* enhance labor-management relations as never before. Rank-and-filers have their own untutored, but no less intense, grasp of these contradictory possibilities, and many experience considerable stress trying to sort it all out—and trying to get out ahead of some of it.

Where labor-management conflict is concerned, the scene has been marked recently by intense encounters of an organizational variety:

• The Construction-Users Anti-Inflation League, chaired by Roger Blough of U.S. Steel, has joined contractors, construction companies, and other businesses in rolling back the percentage of unionized construction done by unionized firms: " . . . a quiet but intense drama is being played out across the nation as building-trade unions try to fight off the invasion of nonunion construction companies. The unions, whose hiring halls once gave them nearly total dominance as labor brokers in the industry, have been unable to halt a shrinking of their labor-force control."[18]

• Deauthorization polls challenging union shop agreements, successful employer refusals to bargain, and decertification elections challenging the unions' status as bargaining representatives have soared in number (the last, for example, went from 124 with 66 percent successful in 1967 to 849 with 76 percent successful in 1977).[19]

• Many consulting firms are thriving as a part of "a phenomenon that is growing by leaps and bounds—law firms and consultants who collect a handsome living by selling expert advice on how to keep the union out or, if the union is already in, how to combat it and possibly get rid of it."[20] Asked about these outfits, George Meany conceded that "they give us considerable concern," and a new AFL-CIO pamphlet on the subject notes "a 250 percent increase in unfair labor practice complaints against employers in the last 10 years, due in part to these consultants."[21]

Numerous other examples could be offered, but the point should already be clear: As seen by Donald Fraser, the president of the United Auto Workers Union, and as conveyed by him and other unionists to their rank-and-file members, "leaders of the business community, with few exceptions, have chosen to wage a one-sided class war today in this country.[22]

However, various business spokesmen view the above conflicts quite differently, as made clear recently by Peter J. Pestillo, vice-president of Corporate Employee Relations for B.F. Goodrich:

> *The trouble for labor comes not from those who hate unions, but from those who have concluded in the most dispassionate of ways that living without a union is a sound business decision . . . in order to remain competitive [we] must remain nonunion . . . we business managers have decided we can run [the union's industrial] justice system better [alone].*[23]

Pestillo adds his conviction that this nonunion development need not upset existing labor-management relationships of a mature variety:

> *So long as that resistance stays honest, temperate and clearly within legal limits, it seems to pose no real problems for sound bargaining relationships.*[24]

Dismissing both antiunion *and* prounion polemics as better positioned in newspaper ads than at the bargaining table, Pestillo concludes that "there is such a consuming 'mutual self-interest' served by bargaining that outside forces can do very little to disrupt it."[25]

Perhaps, and then again, perhaps not. "Mutual self-interest," however, does remain *the* characteristic reality of contemporary labor-management relations. At the level of the workplace, the union accepts a contractual and moral obligation to help maintain certain agreed-upon standards of production. At the level of the international union, the labor organization strives to coexist with a minimum of hassle and heartache, regardless of the occasional theatrics of bluff-and-bluster class-confrontation rhetoric required by passing circumstance (as during an impending union election contest, a contract ratification vote, and so on).

Wherever possible, an international union would rather "cut a deal" than do battle, provided that the deal cuts fairly in both ways and that *all* the parties to it have comparable advantages. Coal industry negotiations offer a revealing example:

Incentive pay plans have always been an anathema to most coal miners, largely because of safety considerations and a lingering bitterness about the pernicious piecework systems that were in effect decades ago. By now that resistance appears to be fading.

Some nonunion operators have already installed incentive programs to boost production. And large union mines are introducing bonus systems—though only with the approval of the miners involved—and the spreading practice promises to fundamentally change coal's labor relations.[26]

Some "permission slips," of course, can indicate desperation more than affirm conviction: For example:

More than half of the country's construction has moved outside union control, despite energetic attempts by the unions to stem the tide through project agreements eliminating featherbedding work rules, and forbidding jurisdictional strikes.[27]

Incentives to collaboration, in short, are sometimes very close to home:

When dozens of Food Fair, J.M. Fields, and Lit Bros. stores in the Philadelphia area closed over the last few years, the 19,000-member Retail Clerks Union Local 1357 . . . lost 4,500 dues-paying members. Faced, as a result, with a $450,000 shortfall in its $1.8 million budget, the union has been forced to lay off 14 of its 25 paid staff members [including all four organizers], seek a $60,000 loan from its international, and drastically cut supplies and donations.[28]

"Mutual self-interest," in short, inclines labor to prefer stress-reducing collaboration whenever and wherever possible, though the deciding factor in this equation remains the willingness of management to see more gained here from labor-management partnership than from internecine warfare.

REFORMS

Here, as elsewhere in every chapter's reform section, I try to stimulate fresh thinking with just a *few* of many possibilities worth attention. For example, where international unions and stressors in the lives of dues payers are concerned, six ideas appear to warrant careful consideration. Labor *might*—

- *Explore the development of new policy-shaping antistress research tools.* A union president has called for human impact studies, to be prepared and discussed among all concerned parties prior to the initiation of any job or skill-threatening major technological change (just as environmental impact studies are carried out in other circumstances).[29]

- *Expand labor's range of services.* The Municipal Employees Legal Services program in New York, a union-sponsored innovation, "could signal the beginning of a new era in which it becomes drastically less necessary to be rich or involved in an exceptional case to get competent access to the best legal system in the world." Clients pay $26 a year, deducted from each union member's paycheck in one-dollar payments every other week. In 1978, over 6,000 members used the service, and clients contacted by a journalist "unanimously praised the service they'd received as both effective and distinctly nonbureaucratic."[30]

- *Explore going where labor has seldom been before.* The 70,000-member District 1199 of the National Union of Hospital and Health Care Employees now offers members "the most significant program ever undertaken by a U.S. union to bring culture to its members." Financed by $900,000 in grants and $350,000 from the union itself, the two-year program will include eleven art exhibitions at union headquarters, a series of four "dialogues" on Martin Luther King's contributions to society (more than 70 percent of the 1199's members are black and Hispanic), twelve evening performances (by such entertainers as Sam Levinson), a street fair, and other events. The most innovative part of the program will have eight dramatic, musical, and poetry programs staged by professionals at some thirty hospitals and nursing homes. Put on during lunch breaks, these programs may reach 15,000 hospital employees (1199 members) and many patients as well.[31]

- *Expand beyond traditional areas of labor scrutiny* to explore increasingly critical matters like equipment design. The president of the Rubber Workers Union insists that "forcing the human body to fit tools, machines, processes—and artificial work environments—that seldom are designed with care for human beings as humans, rather than as living machines, must stop."[32])

- *Encourage academia and media commentators on labor to take a sabbatical year (or more) and get to know union and workplace realities in depth.* Machinist Union president William W. Winpisinger cautions—"The message is: don't tell me what's wrong with me or my job, or what's good for me, unless you've worked with me day-after-day, year-after-year."[33]

• *Explore more outreach efforts*, such as the producing of public relations spots for television explaining labor's side of the story or the establishment of a regular orientation program for new employees dealing with union accomplishments. The steel, aluminum, and can industries, for example, agreed in 1978 to support a two-hour union orientation program for each new worker.[34]

Where progressive employers are concerned, three particular reform possibilities stand out: The parties to a collaborative relationship could—

• *Study the example of the West German government.* "The Germans run a big budget deficit—proportionately bigger than ours. But at the beginning of each legislative session, business and labor leaders sit down with the government and agree on broad wage and price standards that are compatable with the government's plans for growth of the economy."[25]

• *Move to work together to meet the import challenge.* In the past decade, 70,000 jobs have been lost to imports in the shoe industry; 60,000 in color television; 150,000 in clothing manufacturing, and in 1977 alone, 105,000 jobs in steel. A model for labor-industry cooperation on trade reform exists in the Committee to Preserve American Color Television, a coalition made up of four companies and eleven unions, which has been successful in reaching a marketing agreement limiting the number of television sets imported from Japan (prices of American-made sets have remained the same or even declined).[36]

• Expand the *UAW-GM Quality of Worklife Program.* Among its tasks is the development of joint, cooperative experiments and projects designed "to improve the quality of worklife, with an eye toward worker participation in the decision-making process on the job . . . improving the quality of worklife projects helps create a climate in which cool reason and judgment override anger and emotion in working out controversial problems. It therefore has a beneficial impact upon the total collective bargaining relationship. . . . Successful projects (and not all succeed) could begin to alter intrinsically the decades old shop-worn system of management-worker relations and the philosophy underlying the concept of 'scientific management.' It could enhance the dignity of the worker on his job, involve him significantly in the decision-making process, improve the opportunity for heightened satisfaction and move toward a democratization of the workplace not heretofore achieved."[37]

As well, of course, business could reconsider revised versions of 1978's ill-fated labor law reform bill, reject the tactics and intensity of recent antiunion campaigns, and so on and so forth .. on behalf of informed and invigorated labor-management cooperation.

SUMMARY

Rank-and-file blue-collarites look to their international unions and, to a lesser degree, to the AFL-CIO for the valuable stress-relieving functions each type of organization uniquely provides. Some of these expectancies are—

• *Invent new weapons.* Typical of the innovations that ordinary dues payers expect their paid leadership to come up with is the new strategy of putting pressure on union opponents on a board of directors. For example, the Textile Workers Union is asking bankers on the board of J.P. Stevens Co. to force the textile company to revise its antiunion position—or the union will try to withdraw union pension business from the banks in question.[38]

• *Promote new laws.* Typical is a measure that the All Unions Committee to Shorten the Work Week has recently had U.S. Representative John Conyers (D-Mich.) introduce. It would change the federal Fair Labor Standards Act from a forty-hour to a thirty-five-hour basic workweek, ban compulsory overtime, and require double pay for overtime work. The sponsors contend that a shorter workweek would create more jobs by forcing employers to hire more people to maintain production. They believe its eventual passage hinges on labor's success in generating grass roots support, among the rank and file *and* the general public: "With technology wiping out jobs, this is the only way to protect them" explains committee president Frank Runnels, who is also president of a UAW local in Michigan, where the idea originated.[39]

• *Make the best of bad situations.* The Steelworkers Union, for example, has long sought better retroactive adjustment benefits for workers who lose jobs to competition from imports. " 'We will take what we can get,' says John J. Sheehan, the Steelworkers' lobbyist in Washington. Elizabeth Jaeger, international economist for the AFL-

CIO, adds ironically, 'We don't want jobs to die, but if they do, it's nice to have a decent burial.' " [40]

Coursing through all of these and many other stress-reducing functions cited in this chapter are rank-and-file hopes that labor can help make work a little more bearable, supervision a bit more reasonable, the family's purchasing power far more adequate, and the individual's sense of self-worth much more considerable.

Given the fact, however, that the indifference of young workers and the opposition of nonunion employers grows all the time, the scene is becoming increasingly turbulent. Many dues payers regard labor with a hard-boiled blend of studied indifference ("just another racket") and begrudging appreciation ("We'd be dead without it!"). Only this is clear: The stress-relieving functions of organized labor cited earlier—and those explored elsewhere in this chapter and throughout the volume—are *not* readily performed by *any* available nonunion substitute . . . this, a many-faceted contention worth every possible management consideration.

APPENDIX: NONUNIONIZED BLUE-COLLARITES

While a large majority of male Caucasian manual workers are union members, this is not true of a sizable minority in small, rural, new, or Southern workplaces. Their relationship to the labor movement and to blue-collar stress has unique components worth passing attention, if only because some of labor's near future hangs in part on the matter— with all of the stress attendant on that fact.

Nonunion workers enjoy several antistress gains as a direct correlate of labor's hovering and hungry presence. For example:

- Employers intent on remaining nonunion generally match or stay close to prevailing contract terms in relevant unionized workplaces.

- Progressive personnel policies, including speedy and equitable resolution of grievances and sensitive attention to inevitable personality strains at work, are prominent antiunion deterrants.

- Media preoccupation with the crimes of certain notorious union leaders—and with the pain and loss entailed in both wildcat *and* authorized strikes—has some nonunion members relieved to remain outside the ranks.

- Workplace knowledge of union jurisdictional impediments to inter-job mobility and flexibility offends nonunion members who prefer a jack-of-all-trades approach as intrinsically more interesting and more productive.

As well, of course, many unorganized workers are just as pleased not to have to pay monthly union dues to a labor organization—especially when they can persuade themselves that they have it just as well, or "damn near just as well, anyhow."

On the other hand, the nonunion scene includes three major stress-aggravating matters:

- Union organizers, generally only in response to the complaints of a core of aggrieved employees, will put a workshop's situation under an unsparing microscope and compel attention to local employment drawbacks.

- Unionizing campaigns often divide the nonunion workforce into mutually hostile factions.

- Employer responses to the threat or fact of a unionization campaign can exacerbate workplace tensions, undermine employer-employee trust and, ironically, aid and abet the entire organizing effort.

Little wonder, then, that a spokesman for progressive nonunion operations declares that "there is no question that operating on a nonunion basis takes more effort and more sophistication in order to be successful."[41]

Labor's position in this entire matter is impatient and emphatic:

[Employers] are well aware that in an uncoerced environment, the majority of workers will choose collective representation. They know know it is not the employee who feels that collective bargaining has outlived its usefulness.[42]

Perhaps. All that is certain is that the rewards of remaining nonunion will be tested over and again where blue-collar stress stirs a modicum of hope of organizing success, as evidenced by the fact that the number of initial representation elections increased 12 percent between 1966 and 1977.[43]

NOTES

1. "Class Struggle," *The Nation*, January 6-13, 1979, p. 6.
2. Philip Shabecoff, "Union Membership Rolls Queried," *New York Times*, February 1, 1979, p. A-20.

3. Aachary Skear, "The Right-to-Work Lobby," *The Nation*, January 20, 1979, p. 52.

4. *Ibid.*

5. William W. Winpisinger, "Uphill All the Way," *Challenge*, March/April 1978, p. 48.

6. Skear, "The Right-to-Work Lobby," p. 52.

7. David Moberg, "Big Union Turnout Stops Right-to-Work," *In These Times*, November 15-21, 1978, p. 3.

8. *Ibid.* See also "A Key Defeat in Missouri for the Right-to-Workers," *Business Week*, November 20, 1978, p. 41.

9. Doug Ireland, "New York's Mr. Lucky," *New York*, August 15, 1977, pp. 40-45.

10. Bert Cochran, "Machiavelli for the Little Man," *The Nation*, November 18, 1978, p. 555.

11. Fred K. Cook, "Born to Violence," *New York Times Book Review*, November 15, 1978, p. 60.

12. Murray Kempton, "The Pessimist," *New York Review of Books*, February 22, 1979, p. 13.

13. Steven Brill, *The Teamsters* (New York: Simon and Schuster, 1978), pp. 173-174. See also Dan E. Moldea, *The Hoffa Wars* (New York: Paddington Press, 1978).

14. Brill, *The Teamsters*, p. 174. See also Matt Witt, "Two Reform Groups Take on the Teamsters," *Working Papers*, July/August 1978, pp. 10-14; H.W. Benson, "Reform Among the Teamsters," *Dissent*, Spring 1979, pp. 153-157.

15. *Ibid.*, pp. 153-154.

16. Bob Master, "Criminal Code Reform Bill Endangers Workers' Rights," *Labor Unity* [Amalgamated Clothing Workers' Union], June 1978, p. 20.

17. Penn Kemble, "Labor Draws the Line," *Public Opinion*, November/December 1978, p. 20.

18. Robert W. Merry, "Struggle at the Site," *Wall Street Journal*, April 11, 1979, p. 48.

19. Thomas Ferguson and Joel Rogers, "The State of the Unions," *The Nation*, April 28, 1979, p. 463.

20. Nancy Stiefel, "A 'Spy' on Management School Tells 'Secrets,' " *Allied Industrial Worker*, January 1979, p. 10. See also "The Antiunion Grievance Ploy," *Business Week*, February 12, 1979, pp. 117, 120.

21. Jerry Flint, "Legislative Tactics Modified by Labor," *New York Times*, February 24, 1979, p. 8.

22. As quoted in Ron Chernow, "Douglas Fraser: Labor's Courtly Rebel," *Saturday Review*, April 14, 1979, p. 17.

23. Peter J. Pestillo, "Who Needs Unions?" *The Wharton Magazine*, Spring 1979, p. 32.

24. *Ibid.*

25. *Ibid.* Cf. Alan Kistler, "Companies Break the Law to Break Unions," *The Wharton Magazine*, Spring 1979, p. 36.

26. "Coal Miners Relent on Incentive Plans," *Business Week*, August 7, 1978, pp. 31-32. See also David Bensman, "Troubles in the Coal Fields," *Dissent*, Summer 1978. " . . . the fact that the strikers welcomed the incentive plan indicates that the UMW leadership has not succeeded in teaching its members fundamental union principles" (p. 248).

27. A.H. Raskin, "It Isn't Labor's Day," *The Nation*, September 9, 1978, p. 198.

28. Steve Twomey, "Major Store Closings Hit Clerks Union Hard," *Philadelphia Inquirer*, April 27, 1979, p. B-1.

29. Glenn Watts, "The Work Ethic Is Alive in America." *Viewpoint* 8 (1978): 10.

30. Steven Brill, "Lawyers for the Workers," *Esquire*, January 2, 1979, pp. 14, 16.

31. "A Union Crusades for Rank-and-File Culture," *Business Week*, January 15, 1979, p. 108.

32. Peter Bommarito, "We'd Really Rather Stay Healthy," *Viewpoint* 8, No. 3 (1978): 15.

33. William W. Winpisinger, "Uphill All the Way," *Challenge*, March/April 1978, p. 48.

34. Watts, "The Work Ethic, p. 12.

35. Ibid.

36. "Hope for the Import Victims," *Business Week*, July 4, 1977, p. 17.

37. Irving Bluestone, vice-president, UAW, "Improving the Quality of Workplace," unpublished paper prepared for the First National Seminar on Industrial Rights in the Corporation, New York, May 9, 1978, pp. 13, 16. See also Daniel Zwerdling, "Workplace Democracy: A Strategy for Survival," *The Progressive*, August, 1978, p. 18; Irving Bluestone, "Work Humanization in Practice: What Can Labor Do?" in W.J. Heisler and J.W. Houck, eds., *A Matter of Dignity: Inquiries into the Humanization of Work* (Notre Dame, IN: University of Notre Dame Press, 1977).

38. Wayne King, "Union to Intensify Fight with Stevens," *New York Times*, March 7, 1979, p. D-5.

39. Ira Fine, "Labor Panel Aims at 35-Hour Week, Pushing New Bill," *Pittsburgh Press*, April 1, 1979, p. G-1.

40. "Steelworkers Grope for a New Course," *U.S. News and World Report*, October 2, 1978, p. 99.

41. Peter J. Pestillo, "Who Needs Unions?" *The Wharton Magazine*, Spring 1979, p. 35.

42. Alan Kistler, "Companies Break the Law to Break Unions," *The Wharton Magazine*, Spring 1979, p. 37.

43. *Ibid.*, p. 36.

READING:
SPEAKING UP FOR LABOR—
AND THE LABORING MAN

Blue-collar unionists often find the harassment of the vast majority of the nation's editorial writers hard to bear, especially when media criticism seems indifferent to certain hard-boiled realities that profoundly alter the workplace situation. A former student of mine at the AFL-CIO's George Meany Center for Labor Studies, Gary Spencer, recently offered the following corrective to an editorial that he felt simply couldn't be shrugged off.

"Don't Kill—American Dream"

Dear Editor:

This letter responds to another of your myopic editorials entitled, "Labor Day, But Do We Merit This Special Day?" It strives to do two things:

1. To present an unbiased and unpretentious perspective of the actual relationship between "pride and accomplishment," or productivity, of the American worker, and

2. To refute the controvertible editorial comment " . . . the productivity of the American worker has drifted steadily downward."

Although I do not read your newspaper daily, I do peruse it periodically, and I am appalled at the slanderous comments targeted at the working people and the outright perversions and prevarications that abound pertaining to the working class, usually referred to as "labor" or sometimes, "Big Labor."

I would have to concur that, as a whole, workers do not take as much pride in their work as they did "back in the good ole days" (the days of sweatshops, segregation, child labor, etc.). But a truly probing, inquisitive mind will ask, "Why is this so? Why do American workers seem to be preoccupied with wages, salaries and various occupational non-wage economic benefits, while apparently subordinating quality of craft and workmanship?"

One with such a mind will first gather the facts and *then* filter and interpret them through his values. I will now do so.

There is nothing automatic to ensure that the benefits of productivity will be shared with the workers adequately or fairly!! No rules, no regulations, no guidelines, no statutes.

In the 1920s, (again, the "good ole days") rising productivity was translated into booming business profits—but wages and buying power and living standards of the preponderance of the working class lagged far behind. Sales of goods and services did not increase as fast as they could be produced. This led to a very lopsided, unbalanced economy that was responsible for the 1929 crash and the Great Depression. The post-World War II recessions reflected the same failure to convert rising productivity into rising consumer buying power.

Certainly, workers have struggled to keep buying power up with the rapid price increases in recent years.

But wage increases have not been the cause of inflation!! U.S. Bureau of Labor Statistics (Jan. 1978) indicate that the U.S. workers' *real spendable earnings* fell well below the level of 1972, even though productivity had increased by 8 percent in the last five years! And in *real dollars,* adjusted to account for higher consumer prices, buying power of the weekly take-home earnings of the average non-supervisory worker in private industry, after deduction of federal income and social security taxes, *was lower in April, 1976, than in 1965* (Source: Bureau of Labor Statistics survey).

The "average" wage and salary earner (who is he? or she?) constituted the major groups of consumers, as well as the producers, in the economy. This squeeze on the buying power of their earnings poses a critical problem for workers and their families, and it also has a depressing effect on the economy. The "average" worker, even when employed year-round, often cannot maintain a modest standard of living.

Now, the other side, Corporations (that includes the *Abilene Reporter News)* have raised prices much faster than their labor costs have increased. U.S. Department of Commerce data reveals that prices of manufactured goods rose 25 percent faster than labor costs from 1969-1977. These prices have widened ever-growing profit margins.

Output per worker-hour has increased nearly 500 percent since 1909 and has doubled since 1950! On the average, output per worker-hour rose at 2.4 percent per year since 1909, with the rate of increase fluctuating from effects of wars and depressions and recessions.

The major contributors to rising productivity are the improved quality of labor, research and development, new inventions, union pressures and the collective bargaining process, mass production, investment made by business and investment made by the local, state and federal governments.

Now, to summarize, we have two basic premises:

1. American worker *productivity* has *increased* over the years (already quantified).

2. American product *quality* has *declined* over the same time span (not quantified and I will not attempt to do so here).

To these two I will add, and I feel it very pertinent that:

3. The American press (that also includes the R-N) is just as fabricated and distorted as ever in libelling the worker.

Let us once more employ the inquisitive mind and ask, "What is the reason for the apparent incongruities of these three premises?" If the worker is producing *more* for *less* than at any other time in history, why does the press relentlessly denigrate the worker and why are the products he makes of seemingly declining quality?

Could it be that the profit-making corporate world is shamefully wasteful? Could it be that corporations are concerned with company profit *now* and with social survival *tomorrow?* Could it be that American business produces whatever will sell—good, bad or mediocre? It will use whatever resources it needs for the sale; it will attempt to produce as cheaply as possible, regardless of the damage to the environment and its inhabitants? That it does this in a society that equates *profits* with *progress?*

I quote from one of your own, John McCormally, editor of the Burlington, Iowa *Hawkeye,* " . . . There is the inevitable pressure of bigness, and the devotion to profit and to conformity which is the nature of the corporate beast. The good newspaper does things that outrage the corporate mind. It spends money it can't hope to recover covering the news simply because it has an obligation to do so; it deliberately offends good customers; it deprecates all institutions, including itself."

Of the approximate 1,500 American cities with daily newspapers, 97.5 percent have no local competition. More than 50 percent of all daily circulation rests in the hands of 25 newspapers, and 75 percent of all circulation is controlled by multiple ownership.

Armed with that information, we can now add a new "big" to the list of "Big Labor," "Big Brother," "Big Business,"—"Big News."

Finally, the prime reason for increasing productivity is the improvement in the quality of American labor. Educated, experienced, skilled workers are highly productive workers and an asset to the American economy.

To you, Mr. Editor, I say, "The lesson is clear—economic policy must seek a fair distribution of the potential benefits from rising productivity."

Perhaps then, we the readers of the *Abilene Reporter-News* and the working peple and consumers of West Texas and America, will see a *better Reporter-News,* and *better* products on the shelf of vastly improved quality!

Don't completely *kill* the American Dream—its life is hanging by a thread! Give us *all* something *better* to look forward to through our labors.

Yes, We Do Merit This Special Day!

GARY SPENCER

P.S. I will be very surprised if you find the intestinal fortitude to print such a fundamentalist essay.

Gary Spencer was born in Hackensack, New Jersey, in 1953 and had an itinerant childhood as the son of an Air Force pilot. He has been actively involved in many union-organizing campaigns in private enterprise. As a federal government employee, he has served as steward, vice-president, and president of the American Federation of Government Employees Local 2356 in Abilene, Texas.

Mr. Spencer has since made the transition "from the firing line to the pursuit of the academic life." He is a second-year labor-relations major at Antioch College of Ohio, George Meany Center for Labor Studies, Silver Spring, Maryland, and continues to serve as labor advisor for his local.

5

BLUE-COLLAR HEALTH: PHYSICAL AND MENTAL CHALLENGES

In this era of subconscious desires, Oedipus complexes, homosexual urges, and other terrifying human idiosyncrasies emphasized psychoanalysis, who will listen to a voice of protest that there is more need than ever for the recognition of the power and work of the commonplace virtues of common sense, humor, unselfishness, restraint, and honor?

REXFORD B. HERSEY*

Illness and medical care often entail their own considerable array of stressors, and the situation here can aggravate, rather than relieve, work-related strain and pain—a grim prospect well known to wary blue-collarites. While most union members have medical insurance, they commonly use it in a remedial, rather than in a preventive fashion, and they often suspect the quality of the care rendered under its arcane terms. Mental health care, in turn, is in far poorer shape, as is illustrated in part II of this chapter.

I make only one more point in introducing this subject, and that concerns the unique loss of innocence (ignorance, gullibility, naivete?) that now distinguishes the contemporary working class from its predecessors. Blue-collarites with whom I have discussed this subject are

*Rexford B. Hersey, *Workers' Emotions in Shops and Home: A Study of Individual Workers from the Psychological and Physiological Standpoint* (Philadelphia: University of Pennsylvania Press, 1932), p. 265.

nostalgic about the good old days when their ethnic enclave neighbor-hoods had no knowledge of cancer or heart disease. Today these same harassed and anxious men share in a free-floating American paranoia about nearly everything they eat or breathe, with some adults actually succumbing to hopeless resignation ("Since 'they' tell me every god-damn thing's bad for me, I might as well just keep smoking and enjoying it for as long as I've got left").

In the good old days, or so my friends like to recall, patients stayed away in droves, and blue-collarites accepted medical attention only under duress:

> My father [a pressman for the New York Times for forty years] went to a hospital for treatment of an ulcer, but only because the company he worked for had a doctor on the premises who insisted he go to the hospital. None of the neighborhood longshoremen were told by a "company doctor" to go to the hospital for treat-ment.[1]

Accordingly, blue-collar discussion of the health scene nowadays is many faceted, complex, and often contradictory: Satisfaction with undeniable medical gains mixes with gnawing doubts about costs and disparities in the treatment offered the have or have-not Americans. In every meaning of the expression, more and more perplexed blue-collarites ask, "What price health? And why in hell isn't ours better?"

PHYSICAL HEALTH ISSUES

To begin with, an increasing number of blue-collarites worry about ill health "souvenirs" of long and unwitting exposure to workplace medi-cal hazards. While they may feign indifference to their own poor health habits, many often privately know better . . . though some seize on media-inflated stories of medical mistreatment to rationalize their own neglectfulness. And finally, while some look forward to substantial health issue reforms in the 1980s, many remain uncertain about the particulars of the reforms they would prefer.

Health remains very problematic in the life histories of blue-collarites—and much of the uncertainty here is increasingly being traced by worried workers back to their workplace conditions. As indicated earlier in Chapter 1 on "Objective Conditions," workers rank health and safety hazards as their second greatest source of workplace dis-content (behind compensation, on a list of nineteen choices.)[2]

With every passing month, brow-arching headlines bring fresh revelations of work-linked health hazards. Five prominent examples can make the point:

- ". . . years or even decades after a person has stopped working with asbestos, he may come down with an illness caused by the particles lodged in his lungs. Last week [May 1, 1978], in the most dramatic evidence of this slow-fuse effect, the Department of Health, Education, and Welfare issued a warning to between 8 million and 11 million Americans who have worked with asbestos since the start of World War II . . . until current standards of production have been in effect for at least fifteen years, just how big a risk today's 5 million asbestos-exposed workers are taking will remain unclear."[3]

- Leather and shoe workers suffer a 5,000 percent "excess incidence" of nasal cavity and sinus cancer compared to the average. Lung cancer is 200 percent higher among metal miners than other people, and prostate cancer was 248 percent higher than average in cadmium production workers.[4]

- "Health, Education, and Welfare Secretary Joseph Califano gave highlights of a new [1978] study that he said shows that more U.S. cancer cases are job related than was previously believed. Mr. Califano told the AFL-CIO's National Conference on Occupational Safety and Health that perhaps 20% of all cancer in the U.S. is linked to exposures related to the workplace. Previous estimates ranged from 1% to 5%."[5]

- "People exposed to low-level radiation at work . . . may be 10 times as likely to get leukemia as has been thought. . . . the findings might mean that low-level radiation posed higher dangers of other cancers as well. . . . Federal occupational standards list five rads a year as a recommended maximum exposure for workers. . . . One researcher thinks that the dose should be cut to one-half a rad."[6]

- "[At issue] is the threat to the reproductive capacity and genetic stability of hundreds of thousands of men and women whose jobs expose them to substances that can cause sterility or cause mental or physical deformity in fetuses . . . men are susceptible to cell damage from toxic chemicals, and it may be damage to the husband that causes a sterile marriage, a miscarriage, or a deformed baby."[7]

Media attention daily to illnesses and premature deaths allegedly due to workplace exposure to asbestos, arsenic, benzene, beryllium, chro-

Molder, Foundry: Dressed as he normally works, this molder handles silica sand as part of his duties in the foundry operation. Many molders contract silicosis, a disabling lung disease, and suffer severely for decades thereafter.

Photo by Ken Light © 1979.

mium, coal dust, cotton dust, DES, EDB, excessive noise, iron oxide, kepone, lead, methylene chloride, nickel, petroleum distillates, radiation, silica sand, vinyl chloride, and zinc. (" . . . 1.6 million of 4 million heavily exposed workers are expected to die of asbestos-related cancer, or 67,000 a year for the next 30 to 35 years. This is about 17 percent of all cancers detected annually in the United States."[8])

Of increasing concern here, by the way, is research on a type of exposure known as "household contact." One such study presently being conducted concerns 626 wives and the children of asbestos insulation workers who did not shower or change work clothes after work. When their work clothes were shaken out prior to home washing, thousands of asbestos fibers were released into the home climate.[9] *In 1978, a full twenty-four years after* the plant in question closed, one-third of the relatives of the workers were found to be ill with asbestosis (lung scarring).[10]

Comparably grim are certain lifestyle proclivities of blue-collarites that further diminish their health prospects. A concerned physician warns:

> *Even if the estimate that 95% of all cancers are caused by environmental factors is accurate—and there is not good scientific evidence to support this statement—it must be emphasized that the major environmental cancer threat is cigarette smoking, perhaps followed by alcohol consumption.*[11]

Food and dietary practices, especially a heavy reliance by blue-collar families on fried food, synthetic foods, chemically preserved foods, snacks, fast-food take-out fare, soft drinks, and frozen dinners, conflicts with the well-intentioned counsel of nutritionists—but many working-class Americans shrug off such seemingly expensive advice.[12]

On this last point, the contribution that a personal habit like smoking makes to a broader health hazard, much new concern is now being focused. Workers in the asbestos, rubber, uranium, and chemical industries, for example, who choose to smoke run up to ninety times more the risk of lung cancer than coworkers who do not.[13] HEW stirs interest with its contention that industry loses about $19 billion a year from absences and premature deaths due to smoking-related illnesses. Another $8 billion in direct health care costs are also attributed to cigarette use, and tallies of this sort help explain why nearly a third of all companies now have some sort of "no smoking" policy (a ban, a restricted areas policy, a poster campaign, the sponsorship of a

smoker withdrawal clinic, or even cash bonuses for those who quit).[14]
Similarly, many workers share in these statistical categories:

> *One-third of all people 40 years of age or older have never had an electrocardiogram. . . . One-third of all people with hypertension have not talked about it with their doctor for at least a year.*[15]

Consistent with this, blue collar men continue to prefer rehabilitative to preventive health practices and commonly ignore annual physical checkups in favor of unavoidable emergency patch-up visits to their doctor.

Some of this avoidance pattern of my blue-collar friends has roots in a profound "old country" distrust of physicians and hospitals. This is kept alive today in blue-collar ranks by seemingly never-ending medical scandals of one sort or another:

> *Horror stories have become legend: the man whose leg had to be amputated because his cast was too tight, while the doctor dismissed his complaints as the ramblings of a hypochondriac; the woman who had a cloth sack left in her abdomen during surgery; the child who ended up severely brain-damaged because the anesthesiologist was careless.*[16]

Blue-collarites collect and trade, almost as with stamps and coins, current media accounts of harm or error from seemingly proper medical practices such as this one:

- Electronic fetal monitoring during birth, used in most hospitals, can give rise to "false positive" indications of fetal distress. These, in turn, contribute to an annual increase of almost 100,000 unnecessary Casesarian sections, with risks of infection and death to the mother and infant. Because fetal monitoring was "not medically evaluated before it was introduced, its uncertain benefits and potential costs and risks were not brought to light until recently."[17]

As well, working-class men can cite chapter and verse of criminal fraud in hawking ersatz medical aids. For example:

> *Thousands of hearing aids are sold annually to consumers who later find they cannot hear any better with them, a Federal Trade Commission study has concluded. . . . The FTC staff said that many of the purchasers of hearing aids were elderly and poor, and particularly vulnerable to sales abuses.*[18]

Hostility toward exposed or suspected rip-offs in the medical realm is considerable among blue-collarites, a part of a more general free-floating sense of vulnerability in a society few workers claim to understand.

Not surprisingly, then, blue-collarites show up disproportionately in mass movements predicated on distrust of official medical practice. For decades now, workers have joined or sympathized with antifluoridation campaigns, even when the hysterical allegation of "mass murder" or "genocide" by fluoridation has threatened to escalate this controversy almost beyond rational resolution.[19] More recently, many blue-collarites have shown up as laetrile supporters, thereby sharing in a "general attitude that regards technology as more villain than savior, and science as more likely to cause cancer than cure it."[20]

Pulling this all together, then, a three-part combination of the health stressors experienced by male blue-collarites, the unhealthy and nonpreventive health habits of many, and their traditional dread of the health enterprise would seem to make a strong case for reform.

PHYSICAL HEALTH REFORMS

Those who would help improve the blue-collar health scene might consider these options:

• *Employer-sponsored blood pressure clinics, pap test programs, weight-watching programs, nutrition programs, physical fitness programs, flu shot programs, and cancer and hypertension screening.* Health care experts view such moves as a major step forward. Says one: "Even if the exercise and smoking and weight programs don't work on an individual basis, the message is becoming clearer: You are responsible for your own health. Instead of looking to doctors to repair what was once a healthy body, keep your body fit. By emphasizing that attitude on a group basis in the cultural climate of the company, that message is being reinforced."[21]

• *Sharing of corporate prevention resources.* W.R. Goodwin, president and chief executive officer of Johns-Manville Corp., is proud of the fact that "our environmental engineers are often consulted by companies seeking solutions to asbestos control needs. Our information booklets, special reports, material handling information, audio-visual programs and medical reference services are in constant demand by customers and other interested parties. Teams of J-M people have traveled across the country conducting seminars on asbestos and health concerns to provide others with the advantage of the knowledge we have gained."[22]

• *Reconsideration of workmen's compensation practices.* The State Industrial Commission in Virginia is well known for its resistance to paying for back injuries or psychiatric costs. Coverage was recently broadened to include surgery for disfigurement on parts of the body other than the face, but only after a lwayer threatened to "bring in three workers who had been terribly burned and have them take off their shirts." A below-the-wrist amputation is compensated at a minimum weekly payment schedule of $47, while nearby Washington, D.C., pays $99. Virginia has a maximum scale of $187 for 500 weeks' duration while nearby Maryland pays $147 a week for life for the same industrial injury.[23]

• *New joint union-management sponsorship of a health maintenance organization (HMO)*, as in the case of the 1979 Health Alliance Plan of Michigan (UAW and three auto companies). Members pay a monthly charge and receive outpatient care for nominal sums, hospital care for nominal sums, and hospital care at no additional cost. Costs are expected to average about $142 for each employee each month, in contrast to $202 that Blue Cross/Blue Shield charges employers. HMO members, however, are not always able to choose their own doctors. (HEW expects HMOs to triple their enrollments in the next decade.)[20] Note also that the UAW and the nation's three major auto makers, while united in creating their own HMO as competition for the Blue Cross/Blue Shield option, are at odds over the HMO's financing: "For the first time in years, auto manufacturers are saying the workers must either share the costs of the medical benefits program or sacrifice some of the features that have made the UAW plan one of the most generous in the nation."[24]

• *Increasingly extensive involvement by unions with the creation and operation of union health centers and programs.* Typical are the centers established in the early 1950s by the Amalgamated Clothing Workers Union in Chicago, New York, Philadelphia, and St. Louis. Financed by a payroll contribution from employers, the free care or low-cost centers emphasize "preventive medicine" (a concern for early detection of illness, unlimited access to health care services, and conscientious follow-up by the center staff).[25]

• *Vast new testing programs.* For example, experts now recommend that those under forty be routinely tested for glaucoma. "Even though the chances of someone that young getting glaucoma are about one in 25,000, the costs of the test are so low and the value of preventing blindness is so great, that such tests are cost-effective."[26]

• *Pain clinics*, for help in returning patients to normal working routines. Taking an innovative approach to old problems, these centers use new techniques, such as biofeedback training and transcutaneous nerve stimulation, along with such traditional treatments as physical therapy. (A patient relates with satisfaction that the clinic "recognized the mental part of a person. Most doctors don't know what you think. But the pain clinic recognized the irritations that go with the pain.")[27]

• *The post-1970 emergence of a new breed of doctor, the family practitioner.* "Like that vanishing species, the old-fashioned G.P., family practitioners will do everything from delivering babies and setting bones to patching up family quarrels. . . . But unlike their predecessors—who sometimes administered more kindness than medical competence—F.P.'s usually have the skills to match their versatility." Blue-collarites will especially appreciate the willingness of family practitioners to make emergency house calls, and to keep their fees as low as possible.[28]

• *The post-1972 emergence of the nurse practitioner and the physician assistant.* Based in the concept of "physician extenders," these new professionals screen patients, take case histories, administer tests, diagnose simple illness, and monitor treatment for chronic conditions. They save everyone money, and save doctors time; as well, many are willing to work in areas where no doctors will move.[28]

• *The nations first chain of department store dental facilities:* Its founder explains that "now people can have their cars serviced, stop for food, buy toys for their children, and have their teeth fixed all in one place. And our prices are usually 30 to 50 percent below those charged by most other dentists."[30]

• *The fastest growing form of health protection in the United States, the 44 million-member dental insurance plans.* Expected to cover 77 million by 1985, this innovation has grown rapidly from its 14 million membership in 1970.[31]

- *Expansion of the numbers and influence of the ten industrial hygienists newly employed by labor unions.* These specialists monitor and help solve on-the-job health problems of 20 million unionized employees. [32]

- *New research sponsorship plans.* For example, the Rubber Workers Union has had a program since 1972 under which rubber companies are required to set aside 1¢ per-hour-worked to pay for research into potential industrial health hazards. Costing about $1.2 million annually, the university-based research has identified excessive deaths from a variety of cancers among rubber industry blue-collarites. Similarly, the Joint-Labor-Management Committee of the retail food industry has obtained $350,000 from the Society of the Plastics Industry to fund university research into the health effects of meat wrapping. [33]

- *The health self-care movement,* an adult education effort to help Americans take direct action and responsibility for their own health care—where and when possible. In addition to pamphlets and books, the movement has produced a trend to medical instruments, supplies, and kits in homes (equipment in a "doctor's bag," for example, enables oldsters to check heartbeats and blood pressure at different times of the day.) Relevant to the case that can be made for this approach is the fact that our death rate has "undergone the sharpest decline since the advent of penicillin, primarily because of a reduction in heart diseases, due to individual efforts at health maintenance." [34]

- *Employer offers of "well pay," an innovative reform that is the opposite of sick pay.* "Well pay" takes the form of an extra eight hours' wages that a company offers workers who are neither absent nor late for a full month. [35] (The Norton Co. in Worcester, MA, for example, provides additional pay at the end of the year for each of the five sick days employees do not take during the year.) [36]

Especially fascinating in this entire matter of reforms is the emerging contention that our *biggest* unsolved health problems derive from life-style misbehavior: Blue-collar males are challenged thereby to reassess their own smoking and drinking habits along with other such items like their willingness to inflict physical trauma on others or even on themselves. [37]

Blue-collarites are just as likely, however, to strongly resent outright prohibitions on their smoking, especially when these are suddenly introduced by an employer newly concerned with lowering his health care premium costs (or so such motives are judged by many cynical workers).[38] Better collaborative methods of encouraging non-smoking as with pay incentive schemes cointroduced with local union backing,[39] should substitute here for "Big Daddy," heavy-handed prohibitions—in all matters of private sector health education *and* public policy agenda: An industrial physician advises—

> *Many things the individual can't do. If you want clean water, it's not up to you. The individual worker can protest, but he'll protest himself out of a job. We need our society to do these things. If it's expensive to provide a safe working place, and it often is, it's got to be industrywide; otherwise that company is at a competitive disadvantage. But what the individual can do with regard to his own personal environment is important. Let him change clothes before he goes home from a lead smelter so that he doesn't give the lead to his kids. Let him not smoke cigarettes so he doesn't add to the multiple-factor interaction.*[40]

Blue-collarites I know are increasingly sensitive to this interplay. Though many are uncertain which of the two, personal or public policy reforms, should receive greatest immediate emphasis and outlay of resources.

MENTAL HEALTH ISSUES

Blue-collarites appear to share disproportionately in the nation's generally alarming mental health scene:

- "One out of four people is 'emotionally tense' and worried about insomnia, fatigue, too much or too little appetite and ability to cope with modern life. At least 10% of the population suffer from some form of mental illness, and one-seventh of these receive some form of psychiatric care. . . . For every successful suicide, eight others (or 200,000 people) may have made the attempt. For every person who dies of cirrhosis—commonly related to alcoholism and malnutrition—at least 200 and probably 300 people can be classified as alcoholics (10 million Americans)."[40]

- A rare study of jobs linked to stress-related diseases in a typical industrial state (Tennessee) produced a list of the ten most stressful jobs, which weighed heavily in favor of blue-collar occupations: Ranked from most to least stressful, the jobs involved inspectors of manufactured products, warehouse workers, public relations workers, clinical laboratory technicians, machinists, laborers, guards, watchmen, sales managers, mechanics, and structural-metal craftspersons.[42]

The authors of this Tennessee research (sponsored by NIOSH) hope that it will call fresh attention to "forgotten" jobs with "stressful components that may have gone unnoticed, except by the victims, and sometimes not even by them."[43] Unnoticed factors here, of course, involve the worker with inadequate selection, placement, and training for the job, difficulties with supervision, unfair criticism, job pressures, unwelcomed overtime, job frustrations, repetitiveness of tasks, job dissatisfaction, and job monotony . . . to mention only a *few* of the workplace stressors increasingly linked to emotional illness, tension headaches, marital discord, "drug" addiction (alchoholism, excessive pill use, etc.), and other problems.

Workers today often *know* that mental health treatment systems offer relevant help for much of what troubles them:

> *For a variety of reasons—first among them, the cost, but also fears about being defined as "crazy," and the reluctance to probe the past . . . the women and men of the working class do not often seek out psychotherapy. But they are aware of its existence and of some of the basic premises on which it rests. In interview after interview, I heard the evidence of that psychological awareness— especially as it was expressed in their concerns about communication in interpersonal relationships and the kind of parenting they are offering to their own children.* [44]

Television talk show guests, newspaper advice columnists, progressive members of the clergy, and even some coworkers have made blue-collarites aware of the potential in mental health services. Many struggle with profound ambivalence. They are curious about, but are also antagonistic to, the entire matter.

Mental troubles remain stigmatized in the working-class culture, and this is the nub of the matter (though by *no* means all of it). Factory jokes about "shrinks," "nut doctors," and the derogatory like mask deep-reaching anxiety about the loss of control feared in mental illness. As well, the "talking cure" modality here is foreign to their experience and necessitates time committments, financial resources, and communication skills that elude many of them. As if this were not enough, social class barriers to collaboration and understanding between a blue-collar patient and his "shrink" discourage many from starting or, better yet, persisting in a psychotherapeutic process.

Treatment often flounders on the shoals of blue-collar expectations at odds with the middle-class character of psychotherapy.

Workers, for example, commonly look for the sources of mental stress in present-day matters external to them, such as workplace or neighborhood conditions; many therapists focus instead on long past and deeply personal traumas. Workers often hope to gain relief from mental stress by changing an external variable such as changing jobs: In this way, they underestimate the need for self-correction entailed in mental health treatment. As well, many adult blue-collarites are more available for familiar "needles-and-pills" styles of treatment than they are for any sort of talk cure. And finally, certain blue-collar males, especially older men, are often too emotionally entangled in their own family relations to believe they can openly criticize family members as part of their own treatment and still love and respect them.

To complicate things more, many blue-collarites I have discussed this subject with harbor additional intense antagonisms toward the *entire* mental health system in all of its various ramifications:

• Few agree with criminal insanity court decisions that hospitalize those who commit heinous murders; blue-collar men complain bitterly that "the bastards are gettin' away with murder!"

• Few appreciate the inability to get adequate insurance coverage to meet mental illness recovery costs. A specialist here warns that "it is vitally important that any national health-insurance plan acknowledge the legitimacy of psychiatric problems by providing coverage for their treatment equal to the benefits available for medical and surgical problems."[45]

• Few appreciate the notorious unreliability of community mental health facilities; for example, the National Association for Mental Health conducted a telephone survey on a Sunday in 1977 and found that "one-third of the centers failed even to answer their phones, let alone provide the emergency 24-hour services required by law for federal assistance."[46]

Paradoxically, then, many adult male blue-collarites remain alienated from public policy aspects of the modern mental health treatment system, and some even find the system *itself* an unsettling and deleterious stressor.

MENTAL HEALTH REFORMS

Eight items in particular merit careful and constructive attention in the 1980s:

• *Union mental health training* to help supervisors, foremen, committeemen, and shop stewards identify behavioral-medical problems shown through poor work performance. The UAW's pioneering program, for example, "seeks to assure early case-finding; an effective approach and confrontation with the troubled employee, with sufficient motivation to get him to accept help; appropriate referrals to professional sources; and feedback from the treatment sources so that the employee will receive union and management support to facilitate recovery." While the lay participants do not become diagnosticians or therapists, they do learn much of help in and outside the workplace: For example, they learn how to find and train the existing network of fellow workers who already help and counsel other coworkers.[47]

• *Private sector study of the federal mental health insurance program.* The broadest such program in the nation, the federal plan has the government pay an average of 60 percent of employee premiums. In its Blue Cross variation (eighty different plans are available to federal employees), up to $50,000 a year is available to cover a worker's visits to psychiatrists or psychologists; the patient pays the first $100 and 20 percent thereafter. Since 1975, the percentage of costs going for all such mental health treatments has leveled off.[43]

• *Familiarization of key workplace personnel (management and labor) with the services and phone numbers of mental health community resources,* such as AA, Al-Anon, Gamblers Anonymous, Parents Anonymous (for potential and actual child abusers), the Marriage Encounter Movement, and so on.

• *Expansion of lay proficiency.* In an experiment begun in the spring of 1978, some seventy-five bartenders and hairdressers in San Diego, California, attended classes at a family counseling center to learn how to listen when their customers opened up about their personal and intimate problems. The reasoning behind the program was that "while a lost of people can't bring themselves to seek professional counseling, they might be able to talk out their difficulties if only they have the benefit of a sympathetic ear."[49]

• *Expansion of the small number of labor union contracts that provide insurance coverage for inpatient and outpatient psychiatric care for unionists and their family members.* Such coverage exists today in the aerospace, steel, aluminum, can, and other industries.

• *Expansion of the small number of labor union health centers that include psychiatric treatment modalities for their clients.* "What we are talking about here is making a workplace receptive to individual differences and weaknesses; learning compassion; conveying a different kind of atmosphere and message—one which reduces the stigma of mental illness, increases access to service by saying, "We know that people have emotional problems; it is O.K. to have such problems; we want to help do something about them.' "[50]

• *Joint labor-management sponsorship of university-offered preventive counseling groups*. Designed to help adults guide one another through transitions (such as first childbirth, divorce, or death of a loved one), these groups can take the place of elders or close friends missing from a worker's human network. (A proponent predicts that this innovation will secure national interest in part because "nonprofessional persons who have worked through some of these transitions themselves can be nondirectie leaders of such groups."[51])

• *Cost-sensitive extension to blue-collarites of selected corporate mental health services currently reserved for executives*. This includes the services of full-time or part-time psychologists and psychiatrists along with such stress-reducing options as exercise rooms, meditation periods, and biofeedback experiments.[52] (*Time* reports, for example, that many of the 400 major corporations and uncounted small ones with a formal executive exercise program "have begun exhorting even rank-and-file employees to get out there and sweat."[53])

Here again, as earlier in the case of physical health reform possibilities, the optimum agenda appears to be one that will mix individual responsibility (personal reforms) *with* corporate, labor, and governmental responsibilities. If we are to soon earn significant gains here, the worker, his employer, his union, and every level of government are going to have to do far more than any have begun to consider.

SUMMARY

Throughout the 1980s stress levels are very likely to rise where the workers' physical and mental health are concerned. For example:

• ". . . almost every day Westerners learn of new problems associated with the use of nuclear products. Recently, for example, [a study] was completed of lung cancer rates among uranium miners in Colorado, Utah, New Mexico, Arizona, and Wyoming. . . . 146 of 3,300 miners had died of lung cancer. Statistically there should have been only 30 lung cancer deaths."[54]

• "There is . . . a very real danger in liberalizing the legal concept of 'cause' to the point where anyone can successfully claim that regularly exercised performance on the job 'causes' mental disorder . . . If the compensation courts ignore cause in the medical sense and pay the employee for believing that disability is based on a single stressor at work, they do the employee a disservice . . . I do not see this as a major problem at the moment, but I do see it as a *potential* one, in part because of the growing concern about job stress."[55]

• "The United States Clearinghouse for Mental Health Information recently reported that U.S. industry has had a $17 billion annual decrease in its productive capacity over the last few years due to stress-induced mental dysfunctions. Similarly, other studies estimate even greater losses (at least $60 billion) arising from stress-induced physical illnesses. The need for increased competence in stress management is clear."[56]

Discovery of new risks, revisions of safety standards, possibly misguided legal responses, staggering estimates of the toll, eager media coverage . . . all this and more should stimulate many health stressors in the years ahead.

Similarly, the 1980s should host considerable turbulence on the reform front. In the lifetime of many blue-collarites and their employers there was a time when there was no workmen's compensation, no disability insurance, no health fringe benefits, no industrial mental health agenda, and no extension of health care benefits to worker dependents. Today we wrestle instead with the challenge of economically improving the quality of all of these in-place components of the work scene. While we've come a long way, the effort to ensure a still healthier and less stressful worker at *every* level of the work organization is an effort appropriately without end.

APPENDIX: THE ALCOHOLIC WORKER

No discussion of blue-collar health, physical *and* mental, can be complete without some cogent discussion of the granddaddy issue of them all, the entry-level subject that has helped pave the way for all related attention to blue-collar physical and mental health care.

As a national health problem, alcoholism rates third only behind cancer and heart disease. Almost half of the nation's 10 million alcoholics are thought to be employed (less than 5 percent are skid row types), perhaps three-fourths are males, and one-third may be blue-collarites.[57] As employees they are often absent, accident prone, and grievance prone. Most are believed to function at 60 to 70 percent of their potential, and this, in turn, is thought to demoralize many concerned coworkers and immediate supervisors.[58]

Where industrial efforts to curb employee alcoholism are concerned, the scope of company-based programs has grown dramatically over recent decades to include remedial attention to major side effects:

1940s

Alcoholism, plus nutritional deficiencies and liver damage.

1950s through early 1960s

Alcoholism, plus marital discord, financial disarray, digestive and respiratory disorders, and psychiatric problems.

Mid to late 1960s

Alcoholism, plus dependency on tranquilizers and amphetamines, and addiction to coffee, cigarettes, and food.

Present day

All the foregoing, plus interpersonal conflicts, sexual difficulties, phobias, depressions, and so forth.

Unfortunately, evaluation studies have been confined to only the earliest type of programs, and even then, only five or six such studies are presently judged to have had respectable study designs.[59] While very high success rates are reported, often up to 75 percent three years or more after treatment, specialists are skeptical about the quality of data in these studies: "Probably the one most needed improvement in industrial programming is well-designed evaluative research that investigates the success of these programs."[60]

Enthusiasts point out that these programs connect to a worker's job-holding and earnings potential, two of the strongest possible levers for inducing personal change available in our society. As the right to intervene in an employee's self-destructive alcoholism addiction is based on the widely recognized right of an employer to a fair day's work, even addicted workers may concede the legitimacy of antidrug addiction industrial programs (the programs nowadays are called antidrug in recognition of their focus on "hard" and "soft" drugs as well as alcohol, caffeine, nicotine, and others).

The picture today is a very mixed one: On one hand, specialists estimate that over 2,400 of the nation's work organizations presently have a job-based drug abuse program, up from perhaps 100 such programs in 1970. On the other hand, the national campaign remains weakened by insufficient local funding, apathy, and unfamiliarity. Enthusiasts rush to add, however, that there is no existing evidence of any explicit, well-defined rejection of the basics of such antidrug programs. Even the union leaders' suspicions that these are only "productivity scams" seem to be decreasing, and certain major labor unions are actually taking the initiative in implementing antidrug addiction programs of their own!

Especially laudable are several interrelated advances in the oldest employee assistance programs. A new emphasis on early detection is typical here, as is a willingness to undertake constructive confrontation by sensitively trained lay personnel (supervisory *and* union). Programs now focus with accurate documentation on unacceptable or deteriorating job performance as as this sort of behavior becomes evident long before any physical symptom of the addictive disease becomes apparent. Many programs also refer troubled employees to company counselors who refer the worker in turn to appropriate community help resources (medical aid, psychiatry, A.A., marital or familial counseling, spiritual counseling, etc.). Central to this entire effort is a new "bottom line" assumption that replacing a troubled employee is far more costly than helping him rehabilitate himself.[61]

NOTES

1. Jerry Della Femina and Charles Sopkin, *An Italian Grows in Brooklyn* (Boston: Little, Brown, & Co., 1978), p. 74.

2. Franklin Wallick, *The American Worker: An Endangered Species* (New York: Ballantine, 1972), p. 5.

3. Jean Seligmann, "The Asbestos Peril," *Newsweek*, May 8, 1978, p. 66.

4. "20% of Cancer Contracted on Job," *Pittsburgh Press*, September 12, 1978, p. A-1. See also "Study Sees Health Risks to Copper Workers," *New York Times*, April 10, 1979, p. D-6.

5. "Workplace Safety and Health Task Force Appointed by Carter Studies New Options," *Wall Street Journal*, September 12, 1978, p. 2.

6. "Leukemia Is Linked to Small Radiation," *New York Times*, February 22, 1979, p. A-21.

7. Philip Shabecoff, "Job Threats to Workers' Fertility Emerging as Civil Liberties Issue," *New York Times*, January 14, 1979, pp. D-1, D-8.

8. "20% of Cancer Work-related, U.S. Scientists Assert in Study," *Newsday*, September 12, 1978, p. 12.

9. Dr. Enrique Vasquez, "Asbestos—Carrier of Bystander Cancer," *The People's World*, July 22, 1978, p. 3.

10. Seligmann, "The Asbestos Peril," p. 66.

11. Daniel J. Fink (M.D.), "More on Cancer," *Business Week*, November 27, 1978, p. 66.

12. Harry F. Waters, *et al.*, "Cancer and Our Diet," *Newsweek*, July 24, 1978, pp. 85-86. See also Judith Rodin, "The Puzzle of Obesity," *Human Nature*, February 1978. Stunkard's analysis of a 1960 survey of a cross-section of the people living in midtown Manhattan found that the lower a person's socioeconomic status and that of his parents, the greater the likelihood of obesity (p. 43).

13. Seligman, "The Asbestos Peril," p. 66.

14. Eileen V. Kelliher, "Fewer Workers Now Are Singing 'Smoke Gets in Your Eyes,' " *Wall Street Journal*, November 7, 1978, pp. 1, 41.

15. "Healers to Health: Keep It That Way," *Science*, November 17, 1978, p. 726.

16. Gelvin Stevenson, "Why the Drive Against Medical Malpractice Has Failed," *Business Week*, December 4, 1978, p. 8.

17. H. David Banta (M.D.) and Stephen B. Thacker (M.D.), *The Premature Delivery of Medical Technology: A Case Report* (Hyattsville, MD: National Center for Health Services Research, 1978), p. 3.

18. Jeffrey Mills, "Hearing Aid Abuses Report," *Philadelphia Inquirer*, November 19, 1978, p. 14-A.

19. See in this connection Joel N. Shurkin, "Flap over Flouride; Study Disputed," *Philadelphia Inquirer*, December 4, 1978, p. 2-B; Jean Mayer (M.D.), "Don't Believe that Fluoride Study; the Additive Doesn't Cause Cancer," *Philadelphia Inquirer*, October 1, 1978, p. 10-G.

20. Ellen Goodman, "A Fear that Fits the Times," *Washington Post*, September 14, 1978, p. A-23.

21. "Unhealthy Costs of Health Care," *Business Week*, September 4, 1978, pp. 63, 68.

22. As quoted in *The Asbestos Report* (Denver: Health, Safety, and Environment Department, Johns-Manville Corp., Winter 1976), p. 2.

23. Karlyn Barker, "What Is the Value of Four Fingers?" *Washington Post*, April 17, 1969, p. A-7.

24. Reginald Stuart, "Michigan Is a Battlefield over Spiraling Health Costs," *New York Times*, April 16, 1979, p. A-14.

25. "Better Care, Lower Cost at Union Health Center," *Labor Unity* (newspaper of the Amalgamated Clothing Workers' Union), June 1978, p. 11.

26. Stevenson, "Why the Drive," p. 82.

27. "Clinics that Help Curb the Costs of Pain," *Business Week*, July 24, 1978, p. 160.

28. "The Friendly New Family Doctors," *Time*, July 4, 1977, p. 34.

29. Steven V. Roberts, "Not Nurses, Not Doctors, but a New Breed of Practitioner," *New York Times*, July 30, 1978, p. E-16.

30. Shawn G. Kennedy, "Dentistry in Department Stores Put Less Bite on the Customers," *New York Times*, November 11, 1978, p. 25.

31. "Labor Letter," *Wall Street Journal*, October 17, 1978, p. 1.

32. "The New Activism on Job Health," *Business Week*, September 18, 1978, p. 150.

33. *Ibid.*

34. George F. Will, "A Right to Health?" *Newsweek*, April 7, 1978, p. 88. Especially helpful is Gretchen V. Fleming and Ronald Anderson, *Health Beliefs of the U.S. Population: Implications for Self-Care* (Chicago: Center for Health Administration Studies, 1976). ". . . those who might be judged most 'in need' of the movement appear to be the least likely candidates" (p. 54).

35. "How to Earn 'Well Pay,' " *Business Week*, June 12, 1978, p. 143.

36. "Unhealthy Costs of Health Care," *Business Week*, p. 63 (see note 21).

37. I am guided here by Theodore Rodman (M.D.), "Pitfalls of a National Medical Care Program," *New York Times*, December 10, 1978, p. 22-E.

38. A. Kent MacDougall, "Smoking Ban at Work Place a Fiery Issue," *Los Angeles Times*, September 1, 1978, pp. 1, 21, 22. Unions at the Johns-Manville Corp., the nation's largest asbestos producer, "regard the no-smoking rule as a high-handed change of traditional working conditions, unilaterally imposed by the company without collective bargaining" (p. 21).

39. *Ibid.* "Cybertek Computer Products, Inc., of Los Angeles offers its 100 employees a $500 bonus to quit smoking for a year. . . . Merle Norman Cosmetics passed out $40 bonuses to all its employees, smokers and non-smokers alike, in recognition of the difficulty that smoking only during breaks and at lunch in designated places would cause" (p. 21). "Growing numbers of companies are paying their workers to stop smoking on the job—at least 3% of all U.S. companies and 6% of Canadian companies . . ." in "Companies Put Up the 'No Smoking' Sign," *Business Week*, May 29, 1978, p. 68.

40. "Interview with Irving J. Selikoff," *Business Week*, May 29, 1978, p. 156.

41. John H. Knowles (M.D.), "The Struggle to Stay Healthy," *Time*, August 9, 1976, p. 62. Outstanding in linking this to the work scene is F. Follmann, Jr., *Helping the Troubled Employee* (New York: AMACOM, 1978).

42. Margot Slade, "The Stress-Ridden Inspection Suite and Other Jittery Jobs," *Psychology Today*, January 1979, pp. 13, 14.

43. *Ibid.*

44. Lillian Breslow Rubin, *Worlds of Pain: Life in the Working-Class Family* (New York: Basic Books, 1976), p. 26.

45. Roy W. Menninger, "And Some Voices from Out There," *Human Behavior*, July 1977, p. 30.

46. E. Fuller Torrey, "Carter's Little Pills," *Psychology Today*, December 1977, p. 11.

47. Carl T. Rauch (M.D.), "A Labor-Management Approach: UAW's Employee-Assistance Program," *World of Work Report*, December 1976, p. 6. See also Sheila H. Akabas and Susan Bellinger, "Programming Mental Health Care for the World of Work," *Mental Health*, Spring 1977, pp. 4-8.

48. Kathy Sawyer, "Insuring the Bureaucracy's Mental Health," *Washington Post*, April 10, 1979, p. A-8.

49. "Personal Line," *Human Behavior*, April 1978, p. 12.

50. Sheila H. Akabas, "Mental Health Program Models: Their Role in Reducing Occupational Stress," in Alan A. McLean, ed., *Reducing Occupational Stress* (Washington, DC: HEW, December 1977), p. 193.

51. Benjamin Weininger, "Preventive Counseling," *Human Behavior*, December 1977, p. 73. See also William Bridges, "The Discovery of Middle Age," *Human Behavior*, May 1977, pp. 62-68.

52. See in this connection Gerald Fisher, "How to Deal with Stress," *U.S. News and World Report*, November 6, 1978, pp. 65-66; Marilyn M. Machlowitz, "Mental Health Now a Corporate Concern," *Kansas City Star*, April 10, 1977, p. 2; "How Companies Cope with Executive Stress," *Business Week*, August 21, 1978, pp. 107-108.

53. "From Boardroom to Locker Room," *Time*, January 22, 1979, p. 63.

54. James Coates and Eleanor Randolph, "A Town Where the Very Walls Might Be Deadly," *Philadelphia Inquirer*, April 17, 1979, p. 6-A.

55. Alan A. McLean, *Work Stress* (Reading, MA: Addison-Wesley, 1979), pp. 9-10.

56. John D. Adams, "Improving Stress Management," *Social Change Ideas and Applications*, Vol. 8 (Washington, DC: National Training Laboratories Institute, 1978), p. 1.

57. R.T. Forris and D.F. Lindley, *Counseling on Alcoholism and Related Disorders* (Beverly Hills, CA: Glencoe, 1968), p. 7.

58. J.S. Ray, "Alcoholism and Insurance," *Labor-Management Alcoholism Newsletter* (Washington, DC: National Council on Alcoholism, 1973), pp. 1, 8.

59. Harrison M. Trice and Janice M. Beyer, "Job-Based Alcohol and Drug Abuse Programs: Progess, Problems, and Innovations for Industry-Community Relations," unpublished essay prepared for the Office of Drug Abuse Policy, October 10, 1977, p. 8.

60. *Ibid.*

61. Lawrence Barry, "Industrial Alcoholism Programs: The Problem, The Program, The Professional," *The Family Coordinator*, January 1976, pp. 65-72.

6

ENVIRONMENTAL ISSUES AND EMPLOYMENT UNCERTAINTY

The problem with the "energy crisis," and perhaps one reason why we avoid thinking about it, is that it raises painful questions, not just about thermostat settings, but about our entire way of life and about the range of institutions we have developed to sustain that way of life. . . . Every question raises another question, and the questions lead back to another until we uncover our basic presuppositions about what is good, worthwhile and valuable in human life.

HARVEY COX*

In the 1980s, through the convergence of three blue-collar stressors first known separately in the 1970s,—the challenge of environmental protection, of reducing reliance on jobs in military production, and of free-floating job insecurity—much of the record of blue-collar stress may be profoundly altered. Since there is a blue-collar recreational preference for camping, hunting, and deep-sea and freshwater fishing, many such men are increasingly sensitive about threats to the quality of the outdoor environment. Similarly, given their heavy reliance on autos, their increasing anxiety over gasoline and fuel costs, and their concern over recent "doom and gloom" forecasts concerning energy supplies, many workers wonder "What is it all about—this overnight and now recurrent, talk of an energy crisis?" In a related way, the

*Harvey Cox, "Four Big Ones," *Current Social Issues*, Spring 1977, p. 26.

notorious roller coaster character of military-related manufacturing has certain blue-collarites increasingly curious about constructive alternatives. "Is it possible to keep America strong," some ask, "while getting this economy more into 'peace goods,' and less dependent on the sales of 'war goods' here and abroad?"

As these intertwined topics—the environmental challenge, the economic conversion challenge, and the job security challenge—are reforms of existing social issues (environmental degradation and reliance on Pentagon economics) I fold reform discussion in this chapter directly into the narrative rather than set it off as I do in earlier chapters. Consistent with these other chapters, however, I remain preoccupied with the central question job-dependent blue-collarites ask for openers and closers: "How is any of this likely to effect *my* livelihood?"

ENVIRONMENT AND EMPLOYMENT

The central issue here can be put quite directly: Many manual workers fear that environmental protection measures come only, or come especially, at the cost of *their* jobs.[1] Few men of this persuasion believe anyone else gives a damn about the worker and his postemployment plight or much less cares to hear the worker's side of the story before the government takes some precipitous job-cancelling action.[2]

Typical in this regard are the sentiments expressed in January, 1979 by John Henning, executive secretary-treasurer of the California Labor Federation, AFL-CIO, at the first national meeting of opponents of the Clean Air Act. Henning lashed out at "environmental extremists" and government bureaucrats" intent upon "turning the country into a natural park":

> We think it's blasphemous to stop a dam project just because it endangers a type of spider life. The real endangered species is the unemployed worker—no hope, no future . . . [the push for environment protection comes from] the white middle class sector of society which doesn't care one minute about blacks, the poor, and working people. . . . We know environmental protection is not going to be displaced or denied. But our position is that good environment begins with a job.[3]

The Environmental Protection Agency's (EPA) representative at the conference vigorously disagreed and cited survey data which argued that "belief in the seriousness of environmental problems and support for environmental protection cuts across all racial, sex, education, and income groups."[4]

Perhaps. But many blue-collarites know from long and costly experience that certain industries, communities, trades, and regions will disproportionately shoulder the costs and dislocations of anti-pollution programs, and they expect the brunt of it will be felt by displaced blue-collarites. While they understand that new jobs will be created in the antipollution industry per se, they worry that many displaced by environmental protection projects will not gain jobs because of skill differences, location factors, and union jurisdictional lines. As well, many workers suspect that new jobs in the cleanup effort will disproportionately go to technical and professional workers.

Especially between the generations, between young and much older blue-collarites, arguments exist over which way to go in this matter. Many of the younger men are sympathetic to the proenvironment arguments, and a minority of older men are also genuinely aggrieved by the harm being done to their once-favored woodland or lake resort areas. Proportionately more young than older men, however, appear really open-minded in the matter, probably reflecting the relatively greater ease with which younger men feel they can find new work should they lose jobs because of the defeat of a nuclear plant referendum or a sewer permit/building starts controversy.

"Job jitters" mixed with a genuine sensitivity for environment protection comes through in an excerpt of a Studs Terkel interview with a young local union leader:

UAW Local Union President: *The biggest polluter is the thing we produce, the automobile. The livelihood that puts bread on your table. I don't know if the people in the plant question it. I wouldn't want to see all the automobiles banned because they pollute the air. Yet I realize what the hell good is my livelihood if the air's gonna kill me anyway. There are so many priorities that have to be straightened out. I think all this smog control is tokenism, simply that. . . . It's just another gosh damn gimmick. They're not really fighting air pollution, they're not concerned.*[5]

Whether they are, or not, remains an open and perplexing question for many blue-collarites, though just another among scores in this complex area.

Matters are further complicated by the intriguing claims of pro-environmentalists, such as the solar energy proponents, that their unorthodox energy preferences actually support the development of more, rather than fewer, blue-collar jobs:

> Dollar for dollar, an investment in solar energy and conservation creates four times as many jobs as an investment in nuclear power plants, according to a study by Dubin-Bloome Associates, an engineering and planning firm. The firm compared the employment projections of a $2-billion investment in a dual reactor nuclear power plant at Jamesport, NY, with an equal investment in solar and conservation equipment. . . . The solar/conservation spending would create 64,000 person-years of employment. Nuclear spending would create only 16,000. . . . Plumbers, laborers, sheet metal workers, electricians, and carpenters would be involved directly in solar technology installation. Employment would also be boosted in associated support industries — manufacturing, transportation, mining, etc. Solar technology maintenance would become a major new field, with employment opportunities from manager to laborer.[6]

Solar enthusiasts earnestly want labor support as a leading spokesman makes clear: ". . . if there is one organized body capable of the political leverage needed to boost solar energy, it is the American union movement . . . the unions could tip the political balance away from nuclear power and toward solar."[7]

Unions, in turn, grow increasingly impressed by solar's job-creating and job-maintaining potential:

> Ed Carlough, president of the Sheetmetal Workers Union, AFL-CIO: When Jerry Ford said the energy crisis would force a cutback in air conditioning, I jumped out of my chair. Air conditioning is our bread and butter. So we commissioned not one but two studies on where the best bet for the future of the sheetmetal workers was. And their answer was solar energy.[8]

Nowadays, this union sponsors eight field organizers to unionize the unorganized in this field. It also runs a training program to prepare its members for new jobs in solar power and it has produced a film promoting solar power ("Under the Sun"), which tells about the union's involvement in pilot solar projects and also urges solar home heating on contractors and workers. The union is actually going so far as to guarantee the workmanship of solar installations in residences when the work is performed by union members employed under this union's bargaining agreements.[9]

Another interesting example of labor's stress reaction in this environment vs. job security issue concerns the Steelworkers Union and its insistence that it must be possible to preserve *both* steel-producing jobs *and* clean air. Until recently, however, as the union itself acknowledges, ". . . few outside our union or in industry believed this or even paid much attention to our contention."

A breakthrough was hailed by the union when, in the spring of 1978, an agreement was reached between Wheeling-Pittsburgh Steel Corp. and the Pennsylvania Department of Environmental Resources (DER). Timetables were set for installing additional major air pollution control facilities ($28.5 million), contingent on receipt of federal approval and guaranteed loans to provide the necessary financing. Best of all, the agreement settled a $40 million claim for civil penalities filed by DER that could have put the nation's ninth largest steel producer out of business.

The union's part in all of this went back to an earlier and unprecedented meeting between the entire international executive board of the labor organization and the top officials of EPA. The union had complained that EPA's impact threatened blue-collar job security in utterly unnecessary ways:

Steelworkers Union editorial: *Up to now, it's been all too easy for some government and community officials to take the position that if environmental standards cannot be immediately met, the polluting plant should cease to operate. They didn't care how many jobs were at stake. And all too often, management tended to blame EPA for all the industry's ills.*

By the meeting's end, both sides had hammered out a historic "early alert" agreement: Ever since, EPA has advised the steel union long before taking any action in the steel industry.

When journalists later raised questions about the propriety of the union's pronounced concern for the industry's well-being, the union replied in terms of labor's self-interest:

Paul Lewis, Director, District 15, Steelworkers Union, AFL-CIO: *Our union does not exist for the sole purpose of negotiating contracts and filing grievances. We're here to protect those contracts and to protect the industries with which we have those contracts.*

Lloyd McBride, President, Steelworkers Union, AFL-CIO: . . . *perhaps we need government assistance for steel in terms of modernization. If government assistance is used to modernize, then it is our conviction that industry should make a commitment to keep their money in steel rather than using it elsewhere.*

Overall, the steel union expressed fond hope that its new understanding with EPA would prove—as in the Wheeling-Pittsburgh-DER situation —a sound blueprint for agreements that would insure pollution controls *and* jobs while keeping the steel industry viable in the United States.[10]

In situations where new job growth (as in solar) remains distant, and protecting present levels of employment (as in steel) does not seem possible, the stress reaction of workers often takes the form of "cutting a deal." Fascinating in this connection is the 1978 resolution of a ten-year-long, bitter, violence-marred controversy over the proposed expansion of northern California's Redwood National Park. While loggers were finally unable to stop environmentalists intent on the park's enlargement, they did win an unprecedented jobs program, one that has been called "the most lavish employee dislocation program in U.S. history."[11]

When the park's expansion was first proposed in 1968, blue-collarites were in fierce opposition to the banning of cutting 1.5 billion board feet of trees—enough to keep the local loggers and mill workers busy for an estimated thirty years. Typical was this explanation ten years later from an outspoken partisan, a local mayor of a lumberjack community:

If the people want redwood parks, they got redwood parks already. We got state parks, we got county parks. A lotta time you go out there and nobody at all is using those parks. You know what it is? It's a bunch of loud preservationists—there's only about 50 of them—and they're the ones who've forced this [a 1978 expansion in the size of Redwood National Park]. They want to reverse time. They want the buffalo to run again.

Has anyone thought about what this [the national park] is going to do up here? We're not animals. We're not monsters. We're people and this is still America. We have a right to our destiny.[12]

Labor unions throughout the northwest protested vigorously, and rallies of both sides were marked by large, enthusiastic turnouts, and not a little heated argument and confrontation.

A compromise was finally hammered out by Representative Philip Burton (D.-Calif.) in the form of the Redwood Employment Protection

Program (REPP). Under its pioneering terms, workers adversely affected by a proenvironment move are offered several remarkable benefits:

- Previous earnings are guaranteed to displaced workers for five years, including all fringe benefits, tax free.
- If local unions negotiate a raise for the industry's workers, the nonworking blue-collarites in REPP will get it.
- If the displaced workers want free job training to leave logging for another occupation, the REPP program will provide it. If workers secure work outside the timber industry, their benefits will be cut by only half of the new wage for the five-year REPP period.
- If displaced workers prefer a lump sum rather than installment settlements over five years, they can have it or combine both forms of payment.

As well, the Park Expansion Bill was carefully drafted to include a $33 million restoration project, one that is expected to eventually create about 900 new jobs.

Admirers of REPP represent it as a model of lawmakers' reaction to the threat environmental gains may pose to the livelihood of blue-collarites. Critics, however, point out that barely a year after its passage, the FBI and the Government Accounting Office (GAO) are already investigating allegations of misuse by the labor unions and companies involved (allegations that older workers are being illegally routed into REPP so as to take advantage of its benefits rather than being offered a non-REPP downgrade job). As well, critics insist that REPP will cost four times as much as the $25 million estimated on the bill's 1978 passage.

A thirty-eight-year-old timber-faller, a man with twenty-one years experience in logging who was able to find only two and one-half months work last year, offered this more personal assessment of REPP's meaning to him:

> I might go to school and pick up real estate or something like that. The government, you know, they're supposed to have this reha-bilitation program where we can go, but after a year and a half we're still talking about it.

> It's kind of hell to leave a good job. You risk your butt. I come close to getting killed once or twice a year. But I have got a family and you need the money.

> *Where else can you go, where can you make $35 an hour with my education? High school is it. I didn't even finish high school, I went to the 10th grade.*
>
> *Where else [but on REPP] can I make $35 an hour?*[13]

Hailed by some as an equitable and positive stress-reducing response to job contraction, REPP remains damned by others as a financially irresponsible and fraud-vulnerable payoff. Few doubt it will not be watched closely in the years ahead by anxious workers who feel threatened by "Earthday" advances, in and out of the woods.

Finally, this discussion would not be complete without focusing our attention on the considerable union and blue-collar quandary where the endless debate over the nuclear industry, the environment, and job security is concerned.

On one hand, the eagerness to promote and protect jobs has many in the building trades inclined to support new nuclear plant construction. Typical was the participation of blue-collarites and local union floats in the 3,000-person "Silent Majority" pronuclear rally held in July 1977 in Manchester, New Hampshire. Hailed by its directors as a response to a 2,000-person antinuclear rally held two months earlier at the Seabrook nuclear power plant site, the day-long parade conspicuously featured utility employees, electricians, plumbers, and their families from throughout the northeast. Promising many such marches in the future, a pipefitter explained to the press: "A lot of the fellas are unemployed because these projects are tied up in the courts. You're going to see a lot of us out marching on Sundays."[14]

On the other hand, certain blue-collarites are increasingly uneasy about the attendant risks *and* the low level of postconstruction employ. A representative of the United Steelworkers Local 31, Gary, Indiana, explained this at a June 1978 antinuclear rally at the Seabrook nuclear power plant site:

> *Last week we had a conference with delegates representing 130,000 members in Illinois and Indiana. We voted for the first time, after 6 years of the construction of the Bailly Nuclear Power Plant, to oppose that construction.*
>
> *I'd like to say a word about why I think we and others are coming out publicly in opposition to nuclear reactors. For one thing we are committed to a better environment for our members, a better quality of life. The dangers of catastrophe, of a loss of coolant*

accident, the dangers of constant low-level radiation emissions, and the fiasco around waste disposal—these affect all of us.

But just as important is the realization that the labor movement is coming to that there is no way the traditional trade union issues such as the cost of living and the questions of jobs can be separated from an energy policy for this country.

We think the facts will show that the only way to provide reliable power, and the only way to provide more jobs in providing that power, is NOT to go the route of nuclear power.

We know that there are more jobs provided by virtually every other route.

Before closing the union spokesman made a point of reminding the protest rally crowd of the *quid pro quo* that labor expects: ". . . we want every environmentalist to support the labor movement. That means don't cross picket lines. Support boycotts like the J.P. Steven boycott." [15]

Which way the bulk of the nation's blue-collarites will go in these matters—given the divisions in the ranks, the many unanswered questions, the relentless turmoil, and the hard hard-to-predict crisis (such as the March 1979 Three Mile Island nuclear accident)—remains unclear. That stressors abound, escalate, and demand constructive response is as certain, however, as the necessity of the workers to work this through in an open-minded, sensitive, and provisional way. Much blue-collar energy in the 1980s will be concentrated on reducing stress in these pivotal matters—coincident with the nation's massive effort to also come to terms with the environmental challenge.

ECONOMIC CONVERSION AND EMPLOYMENT

A fascinating variation here is available in the campaign of a few members of the small liberal wing of the labor movement to redirect the American economy. This small coalition of union leaders point out that anywhere from 900,000 to 1,500,000 jobs in the private sector may be directly dependent upon our defense industry with a military spending increase between 1976 and 1978 creating some 120,000 new military jobs. But labor leaders condemn all of this as inflationary since it puts money into the hands of workers without expanding the supply of goods they could buy. What is even more, spending on weapons generally produces *fewer* jobs than many alternative kinds of non-military government expenditure.[16]

This provocative and decidedly minority policy was forcefully put in a key speech I heard in Philadelphia on October 24, 1978, following a ceremony during which the 1978 Peace Award of a well-known protest group, National Committee for a Sane Nuclear Policy (SANE), was given to the president of the Machinists Union, William W. Winpisinger. Honored for his union's pioneering advocacy of "Planned Economic Conversion" (PEC), Winpisinger was asked to explain PEC to an overflowing banquet crowd of perhaps 500 blue-collar unionists and 500 middle-class "peace-niks." Contending that America had "lost its rationality and sanity in Vietnam," he argued that America had been laboring too long under the delusion that war preparation was good business and that citizens must be employed *regardless* of the nature of their production:

> If there is to be a national redemption for America's Southeast Asian madness, then it must come from a commitment, on the part of the people at large, to enlist in the cause of averting war, rather than preparing for or waging war. . . . Now we can begin the hard work of solving the moral dilemma Machinist and Aerospace Workers engaged in defense production face—namely, how to reconcile the need to make a living—to put bread on the table—with the fervent hope for peace and an end to the ominous arms race.

Calling for an end to the "roller coaster cycle of defense production," Winpisinger identified the steady expansion of peace-oriented jobs as the *quid pro quo* for union support of arms controls and Pentagon budget cuts:

> After all, if employers are entitled to million-dollar indemnity payments when defense production ceases, employees are entitled to new jobs at wage and benefits levels they've bargained for and depend upon. Unemployment compensation is not the goal of workers and their unions.

Support was urged next for bills HR 11780, Senate 2279 and 2314, and the Defense Economic Adjustment Act, a legislative plan to win steady and successful enactment of PEC.

Winpisinger drew especially loud applause when he explained PEC in these terms:

It is not pie in the sky. It is solar and other alternative energy sources. It is a rehabilitated, energy efficient rail system. It is swift and low cost transportation systems in our metropolitan areas. It is renovation of the infrastructure of our old and expanded housing program to halt the housing cost spiral. It is development of the technology and manufacture of the equipment to clean up our air and water and to prevent the poisoning of workers in their job environment. . . . It is the humane way, the sensible way, the only way to get workers, communities, and even entire states, off the defense dependency hook.

Keen and searching interest piqued shortly after when the union leader reviewed how conversion would ensure more jobs for workers, not fewer, and would contain guaranteed benefits, guaranteed income, and guaranteed job training.

Moving toward his closing comments, the IAM president struck a note he has often struck before:

The critical question that defense workers all around the country must ask today is this: What are we going to do when the base closes, the contract expires or the shipyard shuts down?

The answer is: plan now *for the eventuality.*

Pounding the podium for emphasis, Winpisinger shouted—"It's time to get tough in the name of peace!!!"

As for the ability of manual workers to participate in such a task, the IAM leader was unequivocable:

Don't say it can't be done. It can. From my own experience, I've never met a Machinist who wasn't a better business brain, a better production manager, and a better innovator or inventor than the brass in the front office. I've never met a Machinist who couldn't use his skill, tools, and a creative talent, to come up with a better idea than the boss. I've never met a trade union negotiator or bargaining committee member who couldn't talk turkey to the boss and bankers alike.

It is those skills, those talents, that kind of creativity that will make Economic Conversion work at the local and community level.

The preliminary reform preparation had already been done, he assured an enthusiastic audience:

All the studies have been made that need to be made. All the surveys have been taken. All the needs have been canvassed. All is in order to get on with the enabling legislation for Planned Economic Conversion.

Drawing his address to a close, the union president counseled that "for nearly thirty years, now, the nation has relied on the 'Peace through Strength' formula. It is inadequate . . . we can achieve a greater and more lasting strength through peace, and I suggest the time to start turning the formula around, is now!"[17]

(Relevant here is the fact that some of Winpisinger's friends are known to have warned him that his policies may not only alienate him from more conservative labor leaders, but also from his own fairly hard-nosed rank and file. With rare exceptions, such as Walter Reuther's conversion ideas back in the 1950s, unions have traditionally championed the short-run objectives of jobs and incomes over the idea of any sort of conversion planning. A concerned labor writer notes, however, that while the Machinists' Union, third largest in the AFL-CIO, has generally been considered mainline and conservative in its values, Winpisinger "seems to have strong support at national headquarters and in the locals."[18])

At the closing of the award banquet special note was made of a new executive order (EO 12049) that both calls for community assistance *prior* to the closing of any military establishment and encourages "concerted involvement of public interest groups." Several unions, we were told, have since begun meeting with Pentagon officials in hopes of writing conversion planning guarantees directly into defense contracts. (One such blueprint urges that the planning itself be done by "management-labor committees at each plant, with the cooperation of representatives of the local community.")[19]

Only this much seems presently clear: In the rank and file and labor's hierarchy considerable controversy about this subject is likely to prove one of the major dimensions of the antistress scene in labor affairs throughout the 1980s.

SUMMARY

Unless, and until, legislation substantially reduces blue-collar anxieties over threatened job loss, American manual workers will continue to look skeptically at calls for both environmental control and defense conversion efforts.[20] Disinclined like most Americans to sacrifice economic security for seemingly distant environmental gains and world peace safeguards, blue-collarites ask—"Why me? Why *our* jobs? How do we really know these new controls are necessary? Or Right? Or even adequate?" Current reform efforts in and outside of labor's ranks strive to recast the issues and to use new data and interpretations. But for the foreseeable future, the key stresses here will continue to involve the absence—at least in the eyes of millions of blue-collarites—of substantial job assurance—the keystone of the personal "environment" of us all.

NOTES

1. For a characteristically early and prophetic grasp of the issues, a clear exploration of how the liberal rhetoric of environmental reform was frequently ignorant of the basic survival interests of the working class, see Chapter 23, "Ecological Movements vs. Economic Necessities," in Irving Louis Horowitz, *Ideology and Utopia in the United States: 1956-1976* (New York: Oxford University Press, 1977).

2. "The growth-environment-energy policy area shows sharp and consistent class differences. College-educated professionals, more than grade school and high school educated manual workers, support environmental protection and reduced energy consumption," in Everett Ladd, Jr., "The New Lines Are Drawn: Class and Ideology in America," *Public Opinion*, July/August 1978, pp. 20-23. For a grim discussion of the likely necessity of government rationing of work under any "steady state economics" scheme, see Lester C. Thurow, "The Implications of Zero Economic Growth," *Challenge*, March/April 1977, pp. 36-43.

3. As quoted in David Talbot, "Ecology and Jobs: Industry Confers to Repeal Clean Air," *In These Times*, January 31-February 6, 1979, p. 4.

4. *Ibid.* See also Gladwin Hill, "U.S. Officials Defend Pollution-Law Impact at California Meeting," *New York Times*, January 16, 1979, p. A-10.

5. As quoted in Studs Terkel, *Working: People Talk About What They Do All Day and How They Feel About What They* (New York: Pantheon, 1974), p. 192.

6. George R. Zachar, "Atom Power Limits Job Stability and Growth," *Critical Mass Journal Nuclear Power Primer*, August 1978, p. 7.

7. Harvey Wasserman, "Nukes and Jobs: Dismantling the Myths," *New Age*, June 1978, p. 68.

8. As quoted in Wasserman, "Nukes and Jobs," p. 68.

9. Robert W. Merry, "Labor Letter," *Wall Street Journal*, October 24, 1978, p. 1.

10. As quoted in "Demonstrating That We *Can* Have Jobs and Clean Air," *Steel Labor ("The Voice of the United Steelworkers of America")*, April 1978, p. 16.

11. Lloyd Shumard, "In California, Jobless Redwood Loggers are in Chips." *The Philadelphia Inquirer*, March 24, 1979 p. 12-A.

12. Sam Sacco, mayor of Eureka, California, as quoted in Robert A. Jones, "After a Long and Bitter Battle, A Clear Victory for the Redwoods," *Smithsonian*, July 1978, p. 44.

13. Lloyd Shumard, as quoted in "In California, Jobless Redwood Loggers Are in Chips," p. 12-A. See also "Income Plan Eases Impact of Redwood Logging Loss," *New York Times*, April 14, 1979, p. 6.

14. "Counterattack for Seabrook," *Time*, July 11, 1977, p. 78.

15. Joe Frantz, as quoted in "Conservation and Solar Energy Provide Jobs, Nuclear Power Destroys Jobs." Literature distributed by the Keystone Alliance (1006 S. 46th Street, Philadelphia, PA 19143).

16. Ann Crittenden, "Guns over Butter Equals Inflation," *New York Times*, November 17, 1978, p. 3-1. The data in this paragraph are taken from this report.

17. The quotations above are from a copy of the speech available from SANE (Washington, DC). See also William W. Winpisinger, "The Defense Worker's Dilemma," *The Nation*, May 27, 1978, pp. 634-635; comparably helpful is a speech Winpisinger gave on April 6, 1978, at the quarterly meeting of the board of the Coalition for a New Foreign and Military Policy (available in reprint from the Coalition, 120 Maryland Avenue, NW, Washington, DC 20002).

18. Sidney Lens, "Winpisinger Makes Waves," *The Progressive*, January 1979, p. 19. See also George Vickers, "Nukes Inspire a New Kind of Movement," *Seven Days*, March 24, 1978, p. 11; William W. Winpisinger, "IAM Case for Solar Power Satelittes," *The Machinist*, August 1978, p. 6; Steve Twomey, "Union Head Gets Award from SANE," *Philadelphia Inquirer*, October 25, 1978, p. B-1.

19. Seymour Melman, "Beating 'Swords' into Subways," *New York Times Magazine*, November 19, 1978, p. 104. This is an especially fine source on the entire conversion scenario and its operational details. See also "Conversion Progress Report," issued in 1978 by SANE (318 Massachusetts Avenue, NE, Washington, DC 20002).

20. Helpful here is Jon Conason, "The Importance of Being Wimpy," *Village Voice*, June 25, 1979, pp. 1, 11-15. "Of the men [machinists at a Brooklyn factory] I spoke with, only a handful even knew who Wimpy is. Even fewer cared . . . most were bitter about what they see as the union's failure to represent them" (p. 15).

EPILOGUE: BLUE-COLLAR STRESS IN THE 1980s

> *When the Titanic went down, the lower compartments were flooded first and thus the people in steerage were aware of the real seriousness of the situation long before the couples dancing in the first-class lounge.*
>
> DR. ROBERT J. YOES*

When I reflect back over the stress problems and reform possibilities reviewed thus far I worry that the decade ahead may try blue-collar workplace lives as seldom before.[1] Over and beyond the numerous stressors I have already discussed, certain *additional* possibilities seem likely to hinder our reform efforts—though we are still in a position to determine the outcome we would prefer:

- *Blue-collarites with more years of schooling than workers have ever had* gain annually in their proportion of all manual workers. Past experience suggests better-educated workers (except for that small number who secure highly challenging skilled posts) are bored and demoralized by the commonplace aspects of manual work.

- *College-educated youth may be compelled by job shortages to accept blue-collar work*, thereby bumping many less-educated workers into joblessness, and exacerbating social class tensions and rivalries

---

* Dr. Robert J. Yoes, "Physics from Another Perspective—A Cynical Overview," from a talk presented at Pennsylvania State University, August 1974 (mimeo) (St. John's, Newfoundland, Canada).

(federal projections indicate a surplus of some 950,000 college graduates in relation to the market for graduates betwen 1974 and 1985). These educated young adults may settle for jobs well below their training and aspirations, thereby creating in blue-collar ranks a grievance-prone underclass.[2]

• Workers may grow intersted in *new campaigns for employee rights* as challenges grow to the use of employee files, free speech limits, dress codes, and so on. Professor Alan F. Westin contends that this is going to be one of the biggest issues in the working world in the 1980s.[3] (Proponent David Ewing cites the progressive policies of firms like IBM and insists that honest and ethical managements need not fear employee rights as they can materially benefit from increased employee loyalty and commitment: "In the long run no organization can achieve much at the expense of the quality of life in its offices, plants, and stores. . . . Much more can be done before we need to worry about threatening the ability of managers to manage."[4]

• Workers are likely to seek *greater-than-ever protection from toxic and long-term health hazards at work* (nine out of every ten workers in the United States are unprotected from exposure to at least one of the 163 most common industrial, chemical, and physical hazards).[5] NIOSH, in 1977, estimated that there were only about 1,000 physicians and 9,000 nurses who spent at least half their working time trying to serve 62,000,000 workers;[6] more than three-fourths of the workers in the 1977 ISR national study believed workers should have complete say or a lot of say in workplace decisions involving safety equipment and practices;[7] 91 percent of a 1978 representative sample of Americans felt that employers should be required by law to inform all employees concerned when the employer has "any information that the health of employees is being affected at work."[8]

• Workers, in the aftermath of the 1979 Weber Supreme Court case, are likely to intensify their *opposition to court-ordered personnel practices that help minorities*, but upset long-standing formulas for equity and career building in the workplace.[9] Especially if a recession in the early 1980s exacerbates tensions related to layoffs and job loss anxieties, the insistence on job-protecting traditions (such as the use of conventional seniority yardsticks) fiercely set white male workers against all others — to the detriment of productivity, workplace-related mental health, and national well-being.

Numerous other challenges to reform are readily apparent, not the least of which is the decision employers *must* make about the vigorous anti-labor campaign being carried over now from the stress-marred decade of the 70s. (Typical is the unprecedented effort underway to earn Congressional repeal of the 1931 Davis-Bacon Act, a law cherished for nearly a half century by organized labor.)[10]

Much of this *could* still aid reform, however, *if* we nurtured its positive possibilities, for example:

- Better educated blue-collarites could promote new gains in productivity and indigenous work reforms.
- College-educated "blue-collarites" could also aid productivity *and* advance their own distinct ideas about workplace reforms.
- Employers and workers could agree to improve employee rights as part of broader pro-democratic reforms in the American way of life.

Similarly, substantial gains in workplace safety, and workplace race and gender relations—along with related gains in the issues discussed in the six preceding chapters—*could* help turn the 1980s into a remarkable decade of antistress gains.

To be sure, scores of stressors in the *after-work* lives of manual workers will also cry out for remedial attention. Blue-collarites seem more unhappy about their communities and country, their jobs, and their interpersonal lives today than they were twenty years ago.[11] More revealing yet, the Gallup Poll, in 1977, found manual workers considerably below those in clerical, sales, professional, and business positions in self-estimates of their own general happiness.[12] Anxious blue-collar men I know lead me to believe their *after-work* lives, the subject of my next book, are fully as stressful as anything we have reviewed in this work-oriented volume.

If we are to lessen workplace stress in the years immediately ahead, our reforms will have to impress all with their realism, sensitivity and patience.[13] While pursued in large part in "the hope of wisdom which our culture must acquire for its survival,"[14] these reforms must deal immediately with the specific likes of inflation's toll, *the* single greatest stressor taxing contemporary blue-collar life:

> *A statistic touted as " the single most politically meaningful of the thousands of numbers tossed out by the government"—the season-*

ally adjusted, average net spendable weekly earnings, after taxes, of a married production worker with three dependents, on a private, nonagricultural payroll, expressed in constant 1976 dollars—was $91.42 in 1969, reached an all-time high of $98.04 in 1972, and fell back to $89.58 in April, 1979, almost two dollars less than a decade earlier! Workers' pay has not been keeping pace with inflation, and "with petroleum prices zooming and signs of an economic slowdown becoming more plentiful, the key figure is likely to deteriorate further." [15]

Progress against challenges of this sort requires an imaginitive collaboration among business, government, and the competent and proud likes of my blue-collar contributors—Spencer, Cuvo, and Yunger. For only as blue-collarites finally help *themselves* can we hope to secure reforms that make a difference, reforms that really count. Critical here, of course, is the "bottom line" contention that workplace stressors left unrelieved in their lives ultimately tax the lives of all of us more than any can recall ever having bargained for.

. . . it might be said that the gap between what is and what might be is the "potential energy" that drives all the wheels of society, the only real source of power in the world. Yes, it is a force that is often blocked by habit or social function or turned into personal profit by men filling a private energy gap of their own, but it presses steadily through classes and nations, breaking up the logjams and recreating the structures until men begin to be satisfied that their hopes and dreams are being met with all reasonable speed."

John Platt, *Perception and Change: Projections for Survival* (Ann Arbor: University of Michigan Press, 1970), p. 43.

NOTES

1. See in this connection Norman Eiger, "Labor Education in a Hostile Environment," *Labor Studies Journal* 4, No. 1 (Spring 1979): 25-38.
2. Al Goodman, "Farewell to the Skilled Worker," *The Progressive*, January 1979, p. 37.
3. As quoted in "Big Crusade of the '80s: Most Rights for Workers," *U.S. News and World Report*, March 26, 1979, p. 85. See also Nat Hentoff, "Free Speech in the Workplace," *Inquiry*, November 13, 1978, pp. 4-6.

4. David W. Ewing, "Employees' Rights," *Society*, November/December 1977, p. 111. See also David W. Ewing, *Freedome Inside the Organization* (New York: E.P. Dutton, 1977); Alan F. Westin, "Good Marks, But Some Areas of Doubt," *Business Week*, May 14, 1979, pp. 14, 16.

5. Richard L. Hudson, "Hazardous Duty," *Wall Street Journal*, April 20, 1979, p. 1.

6. "Most Workers Unprotected," *JUD Spotlight on Health and Safety*, Vol. 7, Third Quarter, 1978, p. 3. See also Helen Caldicott (M.D.), "Radiation: Unsafe at Any Level," *The Progressive*, December 1978, pp. 39-44. "Since the latency period of cancer is twelve to forty years and genetic mutations do not often manifest themselves for generations, we have barely begun to experience the effects radiation can have upon us" (p. 44).

7. Graham L. Staines and Robert P. Quinn, "American Workers Evaluate the Quality of Their Jobs," *Monthly Labor Review*, January 1979, p. 7.

8. Alan F. Westin, "Good Marks, But Some Areas of Doubt," *Business Week*, May 14, 1979, p. 16.

9. See in this connection Ron Williams, "Weber Case to Test Private Affirmative Action," *In These Times*, October 4-10, 1978, p. 8.

10. See in this connection A.H. Raskin, "Management's Hard Line: 'Class War' or Labor's Change to Reform?" *Monthly Labor Review*, February 1979, p. 36.

11. Marc Weiss, "Pension Fund Socialism Revolutionized," *In These Times*, January 10-16, 1979, p. 16. See also Dedra Hauser, "The Unions' Hidden Asset," *The Nation*, February 17, 1979, pp. 171-174.

12. *Gallup Opinion Index*, Report #156, July 1978, p. 26. I am presently at work on a book that reviews the worker's after-work life, its stressors, and its stress-relieving prospects.

13. Invaluable in this connection is Richard Sennett and Jonathan Cobb, *The Hidden Injuries of Class* (New York: Vintage, 1973). See also Jeremy Rifkin and Randy Barber, *The North Will Rise Again: Pensions, Politics and Power in the 1980s* (Boston: Beacon Press, 1978); Robert L. Heilbroner, *Beyond Boom and Crash* (New York: W.W. Norton, 1978). Marxist critics will condemn my recommendations as "aspirins" for treating the symptoms of capitalism's cancer; in sharp contrast, Pfeffer's new book on blue-collar stress insists that capitalism is *the* main source of pain, and such pain cannot be ended without a socialist revolution to eliminate the source. Richard M. Pfeffer, *Working for Capitalism* (New York: Columbia University Press, 1979).

14. Lewis Thomas, *The Medusa and the Snail: More Notes of a Biology Watcher* (New York: Viking, 1979), p. 3.

15. David Broder, "An Inflation Figure the Pols Watch," *Philadelphia Inquirer*, June 25, 1979, p. 9-A.

NAME INDEX

SUBJECT INDEX